About the Books

Writers and Readers Documentary Comic Books are Introductions to some of the major thinkers and ideas of our time. Their form pioneers an attempt to bring words and images together and to translate the most complicated information into a simple, readable and amusing story. They challenge accepted educational notions, presenting simplifications that are intelligent and not patronizing.

Originally intended for the uninitiated, experts from all over the world have come to admire and use the series.

We began the series with books on Marx, Einstein and Freud. These provided the stepping stones for future books in history, current events, philosophy, psychology and the biological and physical sciences. New lines of development are continuing.

While the Beginners Series was originally published in England, it is today available in sixteen languages and in many of the world's major cities, from Tokyo to New York.

OTHER BOOKS IN THIS SERIES:

Cuba For Beginners
Marx For Beginners
Lenin For Beginners
Nuclear Power For Beginners
Freud For Beginners
Einstein For Beginners
Mao For Beginners
Trotsky For Beginners
Capitalism For Beginners
Ecology For Beginners
Das Kapital For Beginners

Economists For Beginners
Darwin For Beginners
Food For Beginners
French Revolution For Beginners
Ireland For Beginners
DNA For Beginners
Peace For Beginners
Medicine For Beginners
Orwell For Beginners
Reagan For Beginners

FORTHCOMING BOOKS:

Black History For Beginners
Brain For Beginners
Computers For Beginners
Reich For Beginners
Socialism For Beginners

Anarchy For Beginners
Feminism For Beginners
Architecture For Beginners
Sex For Beginners
Newton For Beginners

© **WRITERS AND READERS Documentary Comic Books**

Writers and Readers

With thanks and love to Christopher, Lucy and Adam... Melinda

LOVE FOR LAURA. THANKS
TO MY FAMILY AND
FRIENDS,,,,,,,, DAVID

Text copyright © 1984 David Smith
Illustration copyright © Melinda Gebbie

Set in 14/16 English Times Roman by Crimson Copy.
All rights reserved under international and Pan-American Copyright Convention.

Published by Writers and Readers Publishing Cooperative Ltd., London.

Simultaneously published in the United States of America and Canada
by Writers and Readers Publishing Inc.

ISBN 0 86316 065 1

A Writers and Readers Documentary Comic Book © 1984

Manufactured in the United States of America.

First Edition

1234567890

About the Author: David Smith is the author of *Orwell for Beginners, Marx's Kapital for Beginners,* and *Who Rules the Universities? An Essay in Class Analysis.*

About the Illustrator: Melinda Gebbie is a painter and political cartoonist whose works have been published both in Europe and in the United States. A new collection of her art is slated for publication in Germany this year.

Contents

Welcome To The "Reagan Revolution"...

RONALD WILSON REAGAN entered the United States
presidency in 1980 promising a stunning departure from
previous policies. He offered an economic strategy so novel it
was dubbed "Reaganomics" — a program for evading the
usual cycle of inflation and joblessness by stimulating business
("the supply side") while assailing bureaucracy, welfare, and
labor with unprecedented energy. Reagan promised to close the
nuclear "window of vulnerability" and assure renewed U.S.
military superiority after "the decline" of previous years. He
rebuked previous presidents for their policies of detente and
coexistence with the Soviet "evil empire," urging a return to
vintage Cold War politics. The means to these ends Reagan
identified as the promotion of nuclear war-fighting
technologies and redoubled commitment to military spending.

At the same time, Reagan promised to cut taxes, balance the budget, and reverse the growth of government. He spoke up for a "return to traditional values" — patriotism, fundamentalist religion, the family — endorsing New Right calls for school prayers, no Equal Rights Amendment for women, no abortions, and fewer environmental safeguards.

Finally, Reagan announced that prosperity is just around the corner — that happy days are here again — that shining, renewed faith in the U.S. economy will be amply rewarded. Sword in hand, the crusading new president promised glory and new national pride...

The whole package was quickly greeted by the media as a veritable "revolution" — the "Reagan Revolution"...

Is This Really New? Is Reagan Unique?

In some ways, not particularly. Although an ideologically militant conservative, Ronald Reagan is no farther right than several other current heads-of-state. Helmut Kohl of West Germany ousted a long-standing Social Democratic regime in 1982 on an anti-welfare, anti-labor, anti-Soviet platform. Earlier, the Swedish Social Democratic Party had been vanquished, after 54 years in power, by a stringently right-wing, anti-welfare party. And Margaret Thatcher's Tory admistration in Great Britain has served as a virtual prototype for the Reagan administration. Elected before Reagan in 1979, Thatcher has proven equally illiberal: "steely" in her opposition to social services (as the media likes to say); determined to assure Western military superiority and committed to reducing inflation by promoting record employment.

Reagan knows who his friends are. After the summit conference at Williamsburg, an interviewer asked him: "Who do you like best?" Reagan replied:

6

Reagan is not entirely unique because he is not alone. The present flight from liberalism, personified by Reagan in the U.S., consists of a general trend in Western nations *away* from the welfare state; *away* from services for the disabled, elderly, and unemployed; *away* from "guns and butter" liberalism. Reagan, Thatcher, and Kohl are virtually carbon copies, conservatives in triplicate.

Reagan and Co. push guns *instead* of butter — and so far, they've been able to have their way.

Liberalism

Reaganism

Voters may not be in love with Thatcher-style reaction, but they are sufficiently disoriented, sufficiently persuaded that old-fashioned liberalism "just doesn't work," that they are open to conservative blandishments. Margaret Thatcher, for example, has shown remarkable ability to sustain Tory popularity even in the face of joblessness unprecedented since the Great Depression. The near-loss to Argentina of the colonial Falkland Islands (the Malvinas) was converted by Thatcher into a sensational propaganda coup — restoring her once-plummeting public esteem.

Reagan, too, shows great resilience in public polls — first falling, as his policies take effect, and then surging forward again.

The problem is that voters see no future in the welfare state — and no alternative besides Reagan's. His Democratic rivals vacillate, shifting from half-hearted liberalism to "neo-conservatism." No clear alternative is posed.

Joblessness, spiraling prices, taxes, and global conflict make voters insecure. They tend to feel that if the welfare state is not the answer, it may be the problem. Skillful politicians, Reagan in particular, offer an ingenious equation:

He promises *more* — more prosperity, security, and freedom — by means of *less* — less government. The irony is that, in the name of prosperity and security, Reagan and his friends have been able to lead the public into higher joblessness, fewer unemployment benefits, and fewer services for the truly insecure.

Meanwhile, taxes have not fallen for ordinary taxpayers. Budgets are less balanced than ever. The State grows wildly.

Wars have not become less likely.

One argument of this book is that, although welfare solves few major problems, abandoning social services is even less helpful. On one point, Reagan is right — old-time liberalism *is* exhausted. But there are alternatives to liberalism which are *also* alternatives to Reaganism.

As we examine Reagan's anti-liberal assault on the welfare state, we will explore several of these possibilities.

Nor is Reagan entirely different from previous U.S. presidents.

Has the economy suffered frostbite under Reagan? It was also blighted under Carter (1979), Nixon/Ford (1974-75 and 1969-71), and Eisenhower (1957). Johnson contributed, too, by floating $20 billion in unsupported paper bonds to finance the unpopular Vietnam war. Even Franklin Roosevelt presided over a serious economic downswing — in 1937 — and Herbert Hoover will, of course, always be linked to the 1929 stock market crash and the ensuing Great Depression.

When "supply-side" budget-balancing proved unworkable in 1981, Reagan reverted to more orthodox Republicanism — focusing on the substitution of unemployment for inflation *á la* Hoover, Eisenhower, and Nixon.

Mt. Rush-To-War

Is Reagan warlike? So were his predecessors. Virtually every president in this century has sanctioned U.S. participation in some foreign war or another.

Democratic presidents in particular have authorized a vast quantity of fighting. Democrats were in power when the U.S. entered wars in Vietnam and Korea (Kennedy and Truman, respectively) as well as both world wars (Wilson and Roosevelt). And the U.S. toppled governments in Brazil, the Dominican Republic, and many other places with Democratic presidents in office.

Reagan's claim that the Soviet Union is ahead in the arms race — that a "window of vulnerability" has opened up — is an unmistakable replay of Kennedy's spurious 1960 rhetoric about "the missile gap." (In reality, the U.S. has always been well ahead in the arms race, and has never relinquished arms supremacy as a strategic aim. This will be shown later.)

Even the Carter/Mondale administration played a formidable military role, despite its human rights talk: reintroducing the draft; introducing the MX missile system; pushing for the deployment of Pershing 2 and cruise nuclear weapons in Europe; sending the Nicaraguan dictator Somoza $50 million between January and July, 1979, while Somoza bombed his own civilian population...

... urging $1 trillion in war budgeting over a five-year period; promoting Rapid Deployment Forces, Stealth jetfighters, neutron bombs, and laser warfare from outer space. Reagan may have embraced these positions so ardently that they seem like his alone — but they were urged by Carter/Mondale first.

So Reagan does resemble his predecessors. Still, Reagan is an extremist — an exaggeration of the norm — virtually a caricature of other warlike, pro-business politicians. In the words of the old song,

TO SAY THE LEAST—
YOU'RE THE MOST!

Ronald Reagan is easily the *most bellicose* of modern U.S. leaders, presiding over the largest "peacetime" expansion the war budget has ever seen. Reagan has sent aircraft carriers, thousands of troops, and zillions of dollars to places such as Central America, Lebanon, Grenada, and Chad — to avert revolution in El Salvador, to overthrow left-wing Nicaraguan and Grenadian governments, to support the ultra-right Phalangists in Lebanon, and to support pro West factions in Central Africa.

Ronald Reagan has been the most *anti-Soviet* President to date, with a penchant not only for decrying "the evil empire" of Communism, but for securing military superiority. Reagan has pushed the deployment of first-strike nuclear weapons-systems directed at the Soviet Union, and "justifies" his saber-rattling everywhere by allegations of Soviet expansionism (sometimes real, but often imaginary).

Reagan has been the *most openly pro-business* president in a decade of Sundays — in fact, since Calvin Coolidge announced that "the business of America is business" in the 1920's. Reagan has made it a *virtue*, the pinnacle of economic wisdom, to give to "the supply side" (business). The result has been windfall capitalization for big business on a giant scale. And Reagan has been far from shy about his business connections — accepting lavish gifts of White House china; throwing white-tie-and-tophat galas with old-fashioned fervor, etc.

Meanwhile, Reagan sponsored the *most recessionary* economic policy since Hoover's in 1928/1929 — a program of bitter austerity for workers and the poor, and of generous aid to big business. More systematically than any previous president, Reagan withheld from the needy ("the demand side") to give to business. Cartoonist Paul Conrad aptly calls him "Reagan Hood"...

Reagan has also been the *most anti-welfare* president by far, slashing countless programs which even Nixon expanded or left untouched...

Overall, "Reaganomics" has yielded impressive results: the highest unemployment level since the Great Depression; the highest poverty rate in nearly two decades; the highest prime interest rate in history (above 20 percent at one point); and vastly higher budget deficits than ever before.

Reagan has also been *more anti-environment* than any other president in memory, rushing (through James Watt and William Clark) to overturn environmental protection legislation while leasing wilderness and coastal lands to business...

Abroad, Reagan has antagonized even his "allies" — alienating countless Europeans over the deployment of Pershing 2 and cruise missiles; angering Argentina over the Malvinas; winning few friends by aiding dictatorships in Central America.

At home, Reagan is highly unpopular among women, Blacks, Hispanics, and others significantly affected by domestic cutbacks and escalated war dangers. Never before, for example, has a U.S. president experienced a "gender gap" of more than three percentage points (*i.e.*, less popularity among women than men, or vice versa). Ronald Reagan — the screen idol, the heart throb of the old matinees — faces utterly unprecedented disapproval from women. In mid-1983, when 51 percent of men liked Reagan, just 34 percent of women found him acceptable — *two women* for every three men; a gender gap, that is, of *17 percent*. And Blacks like Reagan even less.

Above all, Ronald Reagan is the most dangerous world leader. Never before have political figures held as much power as U.S. presidents do. This particular U.S. president governs the use of an awe-inspiring nuclear arsenal equipped, for the first time, with first-strike weapons. Truman's readiness to go to war was proportionately more deadly than Woodrow Wilson's because Truman had access to atom bombs; Reagan's arsenal is deadlier still...and Reagan shows fewer qualms about the *strategic deployment* and *potential use* of nuclear weaponry than any president before him. Reagan's policies — even his whims — are therefore significant for anyone exposed to potential nuclear holocaust.

Starring Ronald Reagan! The U.S. Mystery Hour...

To understand Reagan's policies, it would help to understand his motives. This is difficult, however. Ronald Wilson Reagan is the most Sphinx-like of presidents — far more so than people tend to realize. Even in the best of cases it is hard to distinguish image from reality with a politician, and Reagan is a particularly tough nut to crack: a shimmering mirage fading into the distance as you approach him, a consummate actor married to an actress, an exceptionally private man with a television persona.

Shadow and substance: which is which?

In some ways, politicians are unknowable by definition. It is easy to be gulled. A flashing smile and an ingratiating manner are insufficient evidence about a stranger's character.

Nevertheless, there is a great temptation to feel that you know a politician. This is especially true with presidents — universally known, their names on everyone's lips, publicized for virtually every statement they make. The president seems like public property, everyone's shared political reference point.

With the rest of us more or less in the shade, the president is an Olympian figure — Zeus on the mountain top, hurling thunder bolts and news flashes courtesy of AP, UP, and Reuters.

Everyone is deluged with information about the president — yet almost no one knows him.

It is an illusion to believe that a remote politician — whether Reagan or Carter, Nixon or Kennedy — can be straightfor-wardly understood by a media-taught public. Naturally, politicians carefully cultivate this illusion — after all, their entire success depends on convincing us that they are brave, reverent, thrifty, friendly, trustworthy, etc. But can we believe the image-makers? When a politician speaks, do we hear belief or make-believe?

Some reliable information is available from tape recorded conversations and from intimate memoirs by real confidantes.

But even on this level Ronald Reagan is uniquely hard to pin down. Even people who follow him carefully are sharply divided on the most basic questions. Two of his former secretaries wrote books to explain him, one with the revealing title, "But what's he *really* like?"

IS REAGAN SHREWD OR MINDLESS?

IS HE A GIFTED LEADER OR THE PUPPET OF HIS MILLIONAIRE BACKERS?

IS REAGAN SINCERE OR INSINCERE? COMPASSIONATE OR HEARTLESS?

DOES HE UNDERSTAND THE CONSEQUENCES OF HIS POLITICS? COULD HE *REALLY* BELIEVE IN NUCLEAR WAR?

DOES HE BELIEVE WHAT HE SAYS? OR MOST OF WHAT HE SAYS?

Questions about Reagan *matter*, in part, because Reagan's charismatic finger rests on the nuclear button. Even if Reagan were personally out of the picture, his policies, if not decisively reversed, could still bear poisonous fruit.

YOUR NUCLEAR THREATS ARE KNOWN WORLDWIDE. EVEN THE CHILDREN SHAKE INSIDE.

NOW WHO'S THE MOST POWERFUL ONE OF ALL?

WAR

Although despised by many, Reagan remains an exceptionally resourceful and resilient politician, with a seemingly inexhaustible fund of public good will. Much of the public *likes* Reagan...no matter what he does to estrange labor, the poor, etc.

His image is warm, soothing, reassuring. Why?

Supposedly, the public has grown cynical about politicians. Yet, even now, a shadowy smiling Hollywood actor with harsh rhetoric has managed to win the hearts, and minds, of tens of millions of people. Somehow, Reagan's bitter words fall softly on public ears.

Many people are convinced that beneath Reagan's sunny exterior there beats a heart of arctic tundra; but vast numbers of people show *some* degree of susceptibility to Reagan's manufactured media image. This merits attention in its own right, later. But first, let's see what we can say about Reagan the man — to see what basis *in fact* his image and popularity may have.

In the words of Lear, from Shakespeare's great *King Lear*:

THE FAIRY TALE LIFE...

Even before he became president, Ronald Reagan was acclaimed
by his supporters in unqualified superlatives. Senator Paul Laxalt
from Nevada started a 1976 book with these words: "Ronald
Reagan is one of the great national leaders of our time, perhaps
of any time." A central part of Reagan's appeal is his image
as a man who — in Laxalt's words — "has risen from humble
beginnings to touch the hearts and claim the loyalties of
millions."

Reagan strikes a Norman Rockwell pose — the image of the
earnest young man from a classic small town, handsome and
patriotic with homespun virtues, who rises to political heights in
the big city. In the process he shows that clean living and decency
are better than all the vaunted sophistcation of Washington
lawyers and Georgetown professors...

Reagan portrays himself and is accepted as the hero of a veritable
rags-to-riches story. He claims the loyalties of millions — and
millions of dollars — as his just reward for baseball-and-apple-pie
virtues. The mighty empire is led by a plain man...

The fairy tale starts on February 6, 1911, in Tampico, Illinois, where...

Ronald Wilson Reagan is born!

The proud parents nicknamed him 'Dutch'.

The family name, Reagan, is a corruption of O'Regan. After great-grandfather Michael O'Regan left County Tipperary for England during the famine of the 1840's, he signed marriage papers as "Reagan."

The young Dutch later credited his Irish ancestry for his gift of gab, saying "there's a trace of Blarney green in the blood of every son of the sod."

Jack and Nelle Reagan, Dutch's parents, moved from one small Illinois town to another — migrating from Tampico (population 1,200) to Chicago (briefly), then to Galesburg, Monmouth, Tampico again, and finally, in 1920, Dixon (population 8,000).

Small town life agreed with young Dutch. In his rhapsodic autobiography, Reagan announced that he had lived "the best life possible." His childhood he calls "a rare Huck Finn-Tom Sawyer idyll," full of "woods and mysteries, life and death among the small creatures, hunting and fishing."

OW!

Grimm Tales

The Reagan family was just prosperous enough to send Dutch and his older brother, Neil, to Eureka College in Illinois. Dutch played football, studied little, served as a basketball cheerleader, presided over the Booster Club and the Student Senate, and defeated his friend, the quarterback, for a pretty girl's affections...

After college Dutch became a sports broadcaster on radio station WOC — World of Chiropractic, founded by the eccentric B.J. Palmer — in Davenport, Iowa.

Assigned to cover the Chicago Cubs baseball team in the spring of 1937, Dutch accompanied the Cubs to Hollywood, where he took a screen test. Signed to a $200 per week contract, Dutch became "Ronald Reagan, the Errol Flynn of B-pictures." He played Secret Agent Brass Bancroft in a series of movies, and recalls starring, typically, as a valiant young reporter on the phone saying,

In 1940 the young star married starlet Jane Wyman after a story book romance. (They met on the movie set of *Brother Rat* and did a 9-week vaudeville tour sponsored by gossip columnist Louella Parsons.)

After serving in the Second World War — in a non-combatant role — the screen star returned to his wife and career.

But times had changed. While Jane Wyman's career blossomed, Reagan's faded. He became active as president in the embattled Screen Actors Guild, eventually serving six terms as president. Disenchanted with Reagan's union preoccupation, Jane Wyman divorced him.

Four years later, Reagan married another young starlet — this time one who shared his passion for public life, wide-eyed Nancy Davis.

Ron's career in politics started in 1949, when he spoke against Hollywood radicals in testimony before a government committee. Not until the mid-1950's, however, did Reagan begin to receive a wide hearing. A plum job fell to him —

that of corporate spokesman for General Electric as host of the pioneering TV show, *GE Theater*. Speaking in *GE* factories and at dinners around the nation, Reagan became widely known as a smooth and beguiling speaker, with an ever more conservative philosophy. Starring in four shows a year and hosting the rest, Reagan stayed with *GE* until 1962.

Even Grimmer Tales

What happens next is common knowledge. After briefly hosting the TV Western *Death Valley Days*, Ronald Reagan establishes himself as a political leader. He delivers a fiery, nationally-televised speech in support of Barry Goldwater's 1964 presidential candidacy. Conservative Republicans urge Reagan to seek election himself. He agrees, and becomes California governor in 1966.

After two terms in office, Governor Reagan decides to seek the presidency. His far-right populism comes back into fashion as welfare-state programs generate a property owner's backlash and as the promise of liberalism seems increasingly washed out. Inflation and recession cap the so-called "war on poverty," leaving room for a new war on the poor. Heralding this cause, candidate Reagan nearly unseats the conservative Republican incumbent, Gerald Ford, in 1976. Then, in 1980, Reagan overwhelms a faceless Democrat, to initiate the most far-reaching policy changes since the New Deal of the 1930's — in *opposition* to New Deal policies.

So the fairy tale is complete. The Illinois Tom Sawyer ascends to the mightiest post on earth. From the breathtaking heights of White House power, Ronnie and Nancy feel "dizzy, awed" by their great good fortune.

Accurate in broad outline, the Fairy Tale version of Ronald
Reagan's life is misleading in crucial ways. Tell-tale details which
yield insight into the president and his social base are typically
left out, and the overall impression we receive is skewed: a
Hollywood version of the truth, prettified beyond recognition.
Reagan inaugurated this fairy tale himself, in his glowing, chatty
1965 autobiography (called *Where's The Rest Of Me?* after the
best line in his best movie, *King's Row*). Many publicists blithely
echo this autobiography, and Reagan's innumerable personal
anecdotes have given many people a vague sense of the fairy tale
plot line — in the same way that millions of people who missed
Star Wars still grasp its flavor from the ad campaign.

To see the Fairy Tale in proper perspective, Ronald Reagan
must be carefully scrutinized in his principal real-life roles: as a
salesman, a *star,* a *millionaire,* and a *politician.* Also crucial
will be an examination of his views, values, and supporters.

The Salesman

Viewed from the right angle, Ronald Reagan's life is a non-stop commercial break, punctuated at regular intervals by moments of suspense and editorial comment. Virtually nothing Reagan has ever done has been unrelated to sales. Whether serving *GE*, Boraxo, and radio sponsors; improving box office sales; or selling his image and ideas in political campaigns, Reagan has labored mightily to lure dollars and votes from audiences favored by his presence. This is not surprising when we review his bloodline...

Birth of a Salesman. John Edward ("Jack") Reagan was a salesman most of his life. His second son was born in a five-room flat above the H.C. Pitney General Store, where the elder Reagan sold shoes. By the time Dutch and the senior Reagan brother, Neil, entered college, the paterfamilias was part owner of "Reagan's Fashion Boot Shop." At other times, Jack Reagan worked as a traveling salesman and in sales at Marshall Field's in Chicago.

Neil Reagan became a salesman, too, winding up as an executive vice-president of McCann-Erickson Advertising, one of the industry leaders.

Dutch Reagan faced his first performing challenge in connection with sales. Even now he finds it difficult to speak naturally when reading (from a teleprompter, a 3" x 5" card, etc.). This first emerged when Reagan had to read radio ads for station WOC. Stumbling time and again, Reagan actually jeopardized his job. To overcome this weakness, Reagan concentrated on memorization — something which comes easily to him and which allows him to sound fresh and spontaneous.

The pinnacle of Reagan's success as a salesman came with his efforts on behalf of General Electric. Toasters, coffee pots, refrigerators, freezers — if *GE* made it, Reagan sold it. Of the eight years Reagan spent with General Electric, he estimates that (besides hosting *GE Theater*) he spent two years doing *GE* flack work on the road.

After Reagan's years on "the sawdust trail" for *GE*, speaking about politics as well as products, he remained a loyal *GE* booster — saying, in his autobiography, that "*GE* was a truly good sponsor, a vast corporation, but as human as the corner grocer."

Even Reagan's athletic accomplishment as a salesman merits comment. In one factory, Reagan signed 10,000 photos in two days! At a plant in Louisville, Kentucky, the assembly-line snaked 46 miles in length, like a giant maze:

Reagan was a cheerful salesman, a happy warrior on the *GE* trail: "The trips were murderously difficult...But I enjoyed every whizzing minute of it!...It was wonderful to encounter the honest affection most people had for the familiar faces of Hollywood." And it was rewarding to see the result: "Back in the upstairs office, the reception was equally heart-warming — the execs were ecstatic: they knew how to evaluate the lost production time against a shot in the arm morale-wise."

Later, Reagan was equally diligent in service to Twenty Mule-Team Boraxo. He even plugged Boraxo as California governor — saying, when asked about the bloodshed his campus policies produced,

And then the poor dears can eat cake!

I'll wash it off with Boraxo!

As recently as 1983 Reagan authorized a British beer company to use his picture on advertising billboards.

The supersalesman later went into politics. But political saleability, like his conventional sales ability, derived from yet another source: his craft as an actor. Let's look, now, at...

THE STAR

The Family That Acts Together Acts Like a Family

Acting, too, was in Reagan's green blood. Is it a surprise to learn that Dutch's mother coached a local drama group?

At one time or another Reagan has performed in top dramas as well as melodramas; on the vaudeville circuit; in a Las Vegas night club act; as a television master of ceremonies, and as a public speaker. No major medium — radio, television, film — is outside his range.

When Reagan started his movie career in the waning years of the depression, he was a hot commodity: a pleasant new face with a near-photographic memory, ideal for the assembly-line style of production Jack Warner had developed for his consistently money-making B-movie division. Reagan could memorize his lines as fast as the Warner stable of writers could crank them out. Under director Byrnie Foy, Reagan appeared in no fewer than 20 B-movies in the late 30's — films turned out at blinding speed, with small concern for quality (to put it mildly).

Brass Bancroft, secret agent   Brass Bancroft saves the day   Brass Bancroft stops 'em dead

Even Reagan was dizzied and a little disillusioned by the inartistic speed of B-movie production. "They didn't want it good; they wanted it Thursday." He felt similarly in 1956, near the end of his movie career, when he starred in a movie with Nancy, *Hellcats of the Navy*.

During the Second World War, Reagan served in the Army Air Corps — in a movie-making unit its stars (such as Alan Ladd) called "Fort Wacky." The immortal films this unit produced include *Rear Gunner*, *For God and Country*, and the Irving Berlin musical *This Is The Army*.

The seven-year Ronald Reagan-Jane Wyman marriage produced two children (Maureen and adopted son Michael) and a few movies.

The divorce itself was pure Hollywood: Wyman won an Academy Award for *Johnny Belinda*, then sued for divorce.

Reagan's second dream marriage was another all-Hollywood event. Nancy Davis was a young veteran of eight movies with an impressive acting pedigree. Her mother had starred on Broadway with Spencer Tracy, George M. Cohan, and early film idol Alla Nazimova (who became Nancy's godmother.) Family friends included theater stars Tracy, Lillian Gish, and the Huston family (Walter, Nan, and John). Nancy grew up with a fascination for acting. "In college I majored in drama, of course."

After leaving Smith College, Nancy too performed on Broadway — most notably in *The Lute Song* with Mary Martin and Yul Brynner.

While in New York, Nancy dated Clark Gable — long enough to worry her mother — and acted on television in addition to the stage. Starting in 1949, Nancy made eight Hollywood movies (before her 1952 marriage).

All in all, Ronald Reagan — who stopped calling himself Dutch at Warner request — performed in 54 movies. Who can ever forget *Law and Order? Bedtime for Bonzo? The Bad Man? John Loves Mary? Mr. Gardenia Jones?*.

The calvalcade of Reagan pictures also includes the unforgettable *Cattle Queen of Montana, International Squadron, The Winning Team, Million Dollar Baby, The Girl from Jones Beach, That Hagen Girl, Tropic Zone*, and *Night Unto Night*.

NO, DON'T CALL ME GARDENIA · OR BRASS, EITHER · OR DUTCH · OR RONALD...

CALL HIM A TAXI.

Some of Reagan's films are widely respected, but, on the whole, Reagan's career was lightweight.

Though the Reagans are very sensitive about his reputation — both list, in print, the films in which Reagan "gets the girl!" — the obvious truth is that Reagan was a pleasant second-lead, typecast as the best man at the wedding, the hero's best friend. After the early salad days of Brass Bancroft heroics, Reagan settled into comfortable semi-stardom. Reviewers typically called his performances "casual"...

RONNIE FOR GOVERNOR? WRONG CASTING! JIMMY STEWART FOR GOVERNOR. RONNIE FOR BEST FRIEND.

That's what Jack Warner supposedly said in 1964...

But the pleasant presence which left Reagan unsuited for starring roles requiring magnetism and a degree of quirkiness — the qualities which made Brando, Bogart, Gable, and Tracy so compelling — qualify Reagan beautifully for the part he now plays.

MR. HOLLYWOOD GOES TO WASHINGTON

The public wants a friendly, pleasant, reassuring leader — not a sneering Bogart or Brando on the prowl. Reagan's unsurpassed ability to speak acidly in a quieting voice is a marvelous asset.

Reagan felt unfulfilled as an actor taking direction from others. Yes, he enjoyed the money and the fame.

And Reagan showed all the good sense you might *expect* from a semi-automaton...

I did a lot of things I'm too smart to do now, but in those days I felt if the director asked you to do it, there must be a built-in guarantee that nothing could go wrong. I swam with the villains supposedly shooting at me from a railroad bridge; the bullets, hitting the water six inches from my face, were in reality metal slugs from a slingshot wielded by a prop man riding the camera dolly. I even let them shoot a bottle out of my hand with a slingshot.

Always careful to accentuate the positive, Reagan stresses "I regard acting with the greatest affection." Still, he adds: "If a man is only an actor, I feel he is only half a man — no matter how great his talents."

When Reagan went looking for his missing half, he found a millionaire — a millionaire who represents other millionaires on the political stage...

THE MILLIONAIRE

Vaguely liberal until the start of the Hollywood anti-Communist crusade in the late 1940's, Reagan once credited his shift to bedrock conservatism to resentment over progressive taxation. It seemed hardly fair that a movie star who had succeeded so beautifully should be so strictly taxed.

This concern with his own personal fortune later generalized to a concern for all the afflicted wealthy.

At the peak of his movie career, Reagan commanded the regal salary of $3,500 per week. He grew used to a posh lifestyle, in one phase ringing up monthly $750 nightclub bills at the Mocambo and the Tropicana. But his movie career dwindled to practically nothing in the early 50's...

Salvation came in the form of the anthology series, *GE Theater*. So broke had Reagan been — nearly $18,000 in debt — that he had started a Las Vegas night club act shortly before.

But the offer from the Last Frontier Hotel proved irresistible:

WE'RE NOT NIGHT-CLUB PEOPLE!

MONEYWISE, THE SUGGESTION WAS A BEAUTY!

The G.E. offer was even better: $125,000 a year, soon to become $150,000. The plain man of the people was riding high. Wearing up a lot of shoe leather on GE's behalf, Reagan grew wealthy in the process.

Investments in real estate proved golden for the Reagans. When the stream of television income slowed in the mid-60's after Reagan shifted to politics, the sale of Yearling Row, a 236-acre ranch in the Malibu Hills, kept the family solvent.

Nancy, in her 1980 autobiography, *Nancy*, expressed sorrow over the sale of Yearling Row: "...Ronnie had taken a large cut in income when he left television to become governor. We simply could not afford the luxury of a ranch."

COURAGE, DEAR. PUBLIC DUTY CALLS

Even his meager $49,000 governor's salary (just one-fifth his previous income) did not qualify Reagan for state relief. This did not prevent him, however, from taking advantage of what he later referred to as "my evil loopholes." In 1970, Governor Ronald Reagan paid no state income taxes. This was the man who had said "Taxes should hurt."

Reagan's evil loophole was a tax credit for "agricultural preserves," for which Reagan qualified by grazing 22 cattle on his 667-acre Santa Barbara ranch. Yes, Reagan agreed this was a very modest investment for a man of his means:

"Wanting to at least have a feeling of still being active in agriculture, I invested a relatively small amount of money in breeding bulls..."

What?? Still no baby bulls?

As recently as 1979, Reagan's tax bill for his ranch totaled just $862. If this ranch had been fully taxed at the rate set for an estimated value of $1 million, Reagan would have paid $42,000.

No wonder he's bullish on private property!

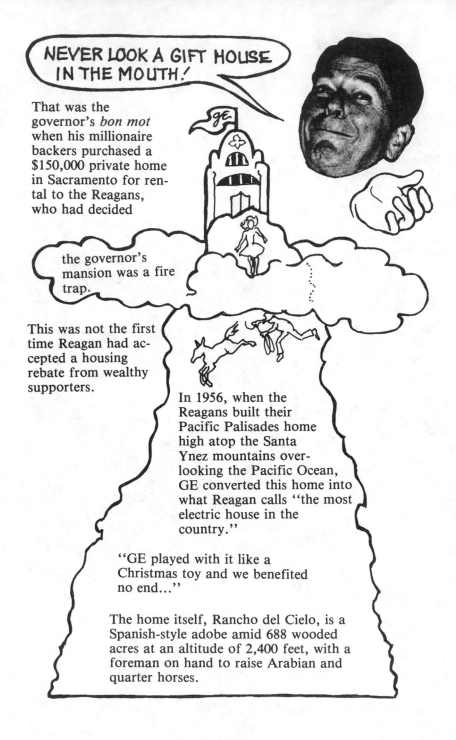

NEVER LOOK A GIFT HOUSE IN THE MOUTH!

That was the governor's *bon mot* when his millionaire backers purchased a $150,000 private home in Sacramento for rental to the Reagans, who had decided

the governor's mansion was a fire trap.

This was not the first time Reagan had accepted a housing rebate from wealthy supporters.

In 1956, when the Reagans built their Pacific Palisades home high atop the Santa Ynez mountains overlooking the Pacific Ocean, GE converted this home into what Reagan calls "the most electric house in the country."

"GE played with it like a Christmas toy and we benefited no end..."

The home itself, Rancho del Cielo, is a Spanish-style adobe amid 688 wooded acres at an altitude of 2,400 feet, with a foreman on hand to raise Arabian and quarter horses.

Reagan's finances soared after he left Sacramento in 1974. In 1975, Reagan made up to ten speeches per month at $5,000 per speech. 174 newspapers carried Reagan's column, and more than 200 radio stations played his taped comments.

Although very reluctant to reveal his finances — so reluctant, in fact, that both the Federal Election Commission and a parallel California agency have sued him to disclose his assets — Reagan did issue a net worth statement in 1975 while seeking the Republican presidential nomination. His total: $1,455,571. More recently, the *New York Times* estimated Reagan's fortune to be in the vicinity of $4-5 million. This total is not surprising if we consider Reagan's late-70's income: in 1979, Reagan reported earnings of $516,000; in 1981, $741,000.

With such stellar income, the Reagan penchant for lavish living is hardly a mystery. In the early 1970's, Reagan grew so carefree about money that he stopped car rying cash all together. (Aide Michael Deaver handles the bills.) As president, Reagan thinks nothing of showing reporters four new pairs of $1,000 boots imprinted in 14-karat gold with the presidential seal — amid the trauma of a recession...

No deficit problem here!

Reagan's path to the presidency was highly unusual.

THE POLITICIAN

Absolutely unpolitical until his mid-30's, Reagan's
first semi-political activity came in the Screen Actors
Guild (SAG) after World War II. Hollywood was
then in a small postwar tailspin which deepened as
television and Hong Kong competition cut into the
market. Reagan shifted his energies to SAG as
employment difficulties mounted.

SAG had been founded in 1933, and it had 15,000
members by the time Reagan ascended to its presidency.
Most were effectively penniless; "the famous men of the
business" who so impressed Reagan when he first walked
into a SAG board meeting were a very small part of SAG
membership.

> Reagan's politics as a six-term union president were
> those of a moderate anti-Communist. He campaigned
> lightly on radio for such Democrats as Harry Truman
> and Hubert Humphrey, but stood out principally by
> supporting the McCarthyite inquisition in Hollywood.

At the age of 43, on the verge of Reagan's start with *GE*, his
political views were remarkably unformed. His marriage to
Nancy Davis had placed him in a conservative context —
Nancy's step-father, Dr. Loyal Davis, was an arch-conservative
who clearly influenced Reagan in this period — and Reagan
was unhappy about progressive taxation. But it was his tenure
as *GE* spokesman that confirmed Reagan as a rightist.

GE president Ralph Cordiner was Reagan's mentor in this metamorphosis. Cordiner, for whom Reagan professes great admiration, felt that Reagan could go places with a definite world-view. He recalls telling Reagan: "Get yourself a philosophy you can stand for and the country can stand for."

GE: We bring good things to life

The ever-modest Reagan agrees with Cordiner that this was the crossroads in his swing to the right...

Is it altogether surprising that the chameleon actor, proud of his corporate connections, soon became an ardent spokesman for corporate interests?

I HAD TO HAVE SOMETHING I WANTED TO SAY, AND SOMETHING IN WHICH I BELIEVED.

Merging a fond concern for business with fashionable fifties anti-Communism, Reagan toured the country virtually without pause. He soon evolved what he refers to as The Speech — the sparkling, crowd-pleasing pastiche of patriotic rhetoric, *Reader's Digest* anecdotes, and semi-facts that rightist audiences have thrilled to for 30 years.

Posing as the scourge of everything unwelcome to free enterprise, Reagan nevertheless accepted guidance from his near-monopoly employer whenever *GE* questioned his rhetorical sallies. Once, for example, Reagan had attacked the semi-public Tennessee Valley hydroelectric power system (TVA) as New Deal "socialism," only to find that *GE* conducted $50 million in annual business with TVA. Reagan promptly withdrew all references to TVA from The Speech.

"MR. CORDINER, WHAT WOULD YOU SAY IF I SAID I COULD MAKE MY SPEECH JUST AS EFFECTIVE WITHOUT MENTIONING TVA?"

This is how Reagan recalls what transpired. Mr. Cordiner asserted.

Another time, for an episode of *GE Theatre,* "we came up with an exciting half-hour play based on the danger to a planeload of passengers lost in the fog with all instruments out of whack."

"We needed someone to remind us that *GE* made those instruments, sold them to the airlines, and said the airlines would consider it tactless if *GE* told umpteen million potential passengers they might land the hard way."

As always, Reagan's primary concern was public safety.

Nancy beautifully summarizes the Reagan doublethink justifying censorship. Sternly, she says, "The very people who criticize censorship are inviting it by not censoring themselves." Excellent, freedom-loving logic! If you step on powerful toes, you have only yourself to blame when you are ground underfoot in return...*nest-ce pas?*

The Jolly *GE* Giant

Reagan, meanwhile, showed the wisdom of paying homage to the powers-that-be. His dinner theater act won immense popularity — so much so that a *GE* executive told Reagan that in the late fifties no one except President Eisenhower was more in demand as a public speaker.

Catapulted into the public eye as an articulate spokesman for conservative causes, Reagan quickly capitalized on his new-found eminence.

At first dramatizing his status as a Democrat supporting Republicans, Reagan finally joined the Republican party in 1962.

Campaigning for Nixon in 1960, and for an array of ultra-right Southern California Republicans, Reagan captured the attention of leading Republican money men.

He was 51 years old. Two years later, as the California co-chair of Citizens for Goldwater, Reagan was invited to campaign for Goldwater on national television — an election-eve speech (October 27) in a hopeless cause — underwritten by wealthy California Republicans to showcase their new star.

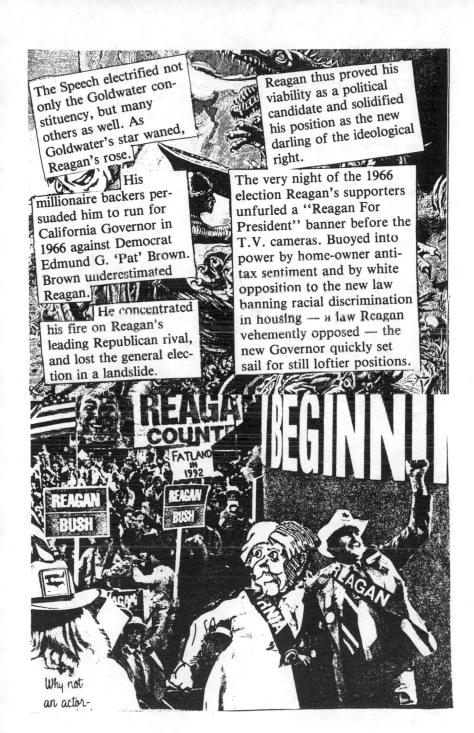

The Speech electrified not only the Goldwater constituency, but many others as well. As Goldwater's star waned, Reagan's rose.

His millionaire backers persuaded him to run for California Governor in 1966 against Democrat Edmund G. 'Pat' Brown. Brown underestimated Reagan.

He concentrated his fire on Reagan's leading Republican rival, and lost the general election in a landslide.

Reagan thus proved his viability as a political candidate and solidified his position as the new darling of the ideological right.

The very night of the 1966 election Reagan's supporters unfurled a "Reagan For President" banner before the T.V. cameras. Buoyed into power by home-owner anti-tax sentiment and by white opposition to the new law banning racial discrimination in housing — a law Reagan vehemently opposed — the new Governor quickly set sail for still loftier positions.

REAGAN COUNT

FATLAND IN 1992

BEGINN

REAGAN BUSH

REAGAN BUSH

Why not an actor-

He was a favorite son candidate for President in 1968, and campaigned actively until it became clear that Richard Nixon was assured victory...Reagan them campaigned for Nixon.

Faced with declining California popularity thanks to his spendthrift budgets and his abrasive disregard for the disenfranchised, Reagan was forced to outspend his 1970 democratic gubernatorial opponent by a giant margin — $3,550,000 to $1,208,000 in the primary alone, without a primary opponent! — to eke out a relatively narrow margin of victory (four hundred thousand votes smaller than in 1966).

After leaving California office in 1974, Reagan once again embarked on a presidential campaign — pursuing, in 1975-1976, "the first real run at an incumbent Republican President, within his party, since Theodore Roosevelt's bid in 1912."

The 1976 incumbent, also a far-right Republican, averted Reagan's challenge but not Democrat Carter's. Reagan then resumed his quest, ran an exceptionally effective campaign in 1980, and became the fortieth U.S. president upon receiving the votes of 26.7 percent of eligible voters (a total of 44,000,000 votes to Carter's 35,500,000).

"All the world's a stage"...and Ronald Reagan is now the leading actor.

RONALD REAGAN
ENTERPRISES LTD.

So, in the nuclear age, the world's most powerful nation is guided by a professional actor — a veritable modern Hamlet, posing the nuclear question...

"To be, or not to be?"

HAM IT UP!

This is indeed the question. Given our fragile global balance, it is perhaps worth asking who writes Reagan's script. If Punch and Judy are on the verge of warfare — who pulls the strings, and to what end?

Abundant evidence indicates that Ronald Reagan is, in large part, a public spokesperson for views and policies formulated by others.

Since the 1930's, Ronald Reagan has spoken lines written by others. Unhappy though he may have been as an acting "automaton," Reagan has never entirely abandoned his early habits.

When he started his campaign for California governor in 1965, Reagan was woefully ill-prepared for the discussion of policy issues. His barn-burning 1964 television speech had been a great success, but it also represented the sum total of his knowledge about public issues.

It was "the same speech," said Reagan, which had served admirably "for six years during the Eisenhower administration" and for four years afterwards, winning Reagan renown. Suddenly, though, it proved inadequate for Reagan's stepped-up speaking obligations.

Anti-Communist cliches were fine for whistle-stop oratory, but insufficient for question-and-answer sessions with the press. Once again, Reagan needed something to say. The millionaire king-makers who had enlisted him for the governor's race supplied the answer: the services of a specialist firm, Behavior Science Corporation (BASICO), run by...

Dr. Stanley Plog of UCLA and Dr. Kenneth Holden of San Fernando Valley College.

Plog and Holden, both psychologists, were given a two-fold assignment: to supply Reagan with information, and to tell him which issues the voters cared about most.

Dr. Holden was later understandably proud that, with BASICO help, the Reagan team "looked at the campaign as a problem in human behavior, a very complex problem." This, according to Holden, was unprecedented...

Ivan Pavlov   John B. Watson

Plog and Holden analysed Reagan's basic speech, identifying 17 key issues which they assigned assistants to research. "We needed statistics to buttress Reagan's ideas," said Plog — and they provided quotations, too, from eminent philosophers and pundits.

WE WERE HIRED...TO GET MORE INFORMATIONAL INPUT INTO REAGAN'S SPEECHES AND TO PROVIDE A PHILOSOPHICAL AND HISTORICAL FRAMEWORK FOR HIS BELIEFS.

"You should have seen those newspapermen jump when Ron first quoted Jefferson to them," laughed Holden afterwards.

As Washington Post columnist David Broder commented, this was "a sort of wisdom-by-association technique..."

Plog and Holden prepared eight binders full of facts and quotes on 5" × 8" cards, which Reagan then used as the basis for his 3" × 5" speechmaking cards...

As if all this were insufficient — leaving nothing to chance — either Plog or Holden accompanied Reagan on every public tour he took for six months, never leaving his side. If questions came up that Reagan felt unable to handle, he conferred briefly with his experts.

Though this saved Reagan considerable embarrassment, he still resented the inference many journalists drew that he was a walking, talking ventriloquist's dummy (an impression not lessened by Edgar Bergen's help during the campaign.)

"That mouthpiece thing bothered him throughout the campaign because he had been doing his own research for years; he took us to his house and showed us piles of clippings in boxes, and he was pretty proud of his collection."

Upon his election, Reagan once again found himself in unfamiliar surroundings....

Campaign manager Lynn Nofziger points out just how innocent Reagan was at this point...

RONALD REAGAN... DIDN'T EVEN RUN HIS OWN CAMPAIGN. HIS CAMPAIGN WAS RUN BY HIRED PEOPLE WHO THEN WALKED AWAY AND LEFT IT. THEREFORE, WHEN HE WAS ELECTED, THE BIG QUESTION WAS, MY GOD, WHAT DO WE DO NOW?

Once again Reagan's millionaire backers supplied an answer. At Reagan's request they nominated people to fill 40 staff positions; all but a few of Reagan's major appointments were made this way.

Even Reagan's most loyal staffers are unable to say unequivocally that Reagan played an important part in formulating policy. Edwin Meese tries:

I THINK HE LOOKED FOR PEOPLE WHO HAD IDEAS AND (THAT HE) ACTED ON THOSE IDEAS AS THEY CAME BEFORE HIM. BUT HE ALSO ORIGINATED A LOT OF IDEAS HIMSELF...I CAN'T REMEMBER SPECIFIC IDEAS, BUT HE WOULD SAY, 'I'VE BEEN THINKING ABOUT THIS. WHAT DO YOU THINK OF THAT? HE DEVELOPED A LOT OF IDEAS HIMSELF, WAYS OF DOING THINGS, SPECIFIC PROGRAMS. I WISH I COULD REMEMBER ALL OF THEM BUT IT WAS NOT UNUSUAL FOR HIM TO COME IN CLUTCHING A MAGAZINE...SAYING 'WHAT ABOUT THIS, LET'S SEE IF WE CAN'T DO THAT!

Reporters who study the Reagan archives on the Stanford campus find little evidence to support Meese's claim. Reams of inter-office memos reveal "an administration full of controversy and rich in ideas."

Bill Boyarsky: "But Reagan initiated few of them."

54

Says 1976 campaign manager John Sears:

"He's not a stupid man. He appreciates the nuances of what is proposed to him. It's just that he's not the originator of ideas...He's not a conceptualizer. He's a borrower and endorser."

A key 1976 speechwriter, Jeffrey Bell, found that

"Reagan had absolutely nothing to say, so I hit on decentralization as his vision of the future."

D IS FOR... DECENTRALIZATION! ENDORSE IT!

There is absolutely no question that Reagan has long-standing views which are really his: antagonism to Soviet Russia, faith in capitalism, hostility to "bleeding hearts" and "freeloaders"... But the specifics of Reagan's policies are more likely to emerge from his advisors than from the President himself. He has no fixed moorings in any particular program, just a bias in favor of right-wing solutions.

EXIT STAGE RIGHT

To discover the source and nature of Reagan's predispositions, we will examine several items: the people who influence him; the views which motivate him; and the policies he defends.

We'll start with the group of advisors who, until dubbed "the Kitchen Cabinet," were called...

The Millionaire Backers

" WE IN THE REPUBLICAN PARTY... HAVEN'T BEEN ABLE TO SHAKE THE IMAGE THE LIBERALS CREATED FOR US 40 YEARS AGO, THE FAT-CAT IMAGE WITH DOLLAR-SIGNS ON OUR VESTS. "

This was Reagan's complaint in the mid-70's, at a time when the Republicans did, indeed, suffer from the traditional Carnegie-Rockefeller image. An early 1975 poll by pollster Robert Teeter showed that most U.S. citizens "thought of the Republican Party as untrustworthy, incompetent, and closely allied with big business." Only 18 percent of the public identified with the Republican Party, and the situation appeared to be worsening.

Ronald Reagan already had a far better reputation than his party. In January, 1976, just 21 percent of those polled considered Reagan anti-worker. Soon, Reagan perfected a new approach to Republican cam-

paigning which eventuated, in 1980, in a rejuvenated image for the party in general.

Impressed by the apparent grassroots populism of Reaganite anti-government rhetoric, the image of fat-cat Republicanism began to fade...

and fade still further...

After embracing *GE* and showing the drawing power of his salty after-dinner patter, Reagan was courted by a variety of would-be king-makers. Nancy reports that in the early 1960's Reagan was asked to run for the U.S. Senate (twice) and the governorship (once).

In 1964 he became the State co-chairman of the Citizens for Goldwater Committee and spoke all over the state in Barry's behalf. A group of prominent Republicans asked him to speak on national television if they raised the money. We didn't know it at the time but that TV speech would change our lives.

And our lives, as well.

Reagan was such a smash success that his business patrons rallied to form a political campaign committee on his behalf, "The Friends of Ronald Reagan." After minor arm-twisting, Reagan was talked into a try for the governorship.

Who sponsored Reagan? The answer is a roll call of the wealthy Goldwater constituency in industry-rich California:

A.C. Rubel, Chairman of the Board, Union Oil Company.

Henry Salvatori, an oil developer, founder of the Western Geophysical Company.

Holmes Tuttle, owner of Holmes Tuttle Enterprises, Holmes Tuttle Ford, two other Ford dealerships, and a director of Rexall Drug and Chemical Company.

These were the prime movers and shakers at the start.

"Friends of Ronald Reagan" set up shop in Rubel's Union Oil headquarters in downtown Los Angleles. Their view, as Rubel put it, is that "Reagan is the man who can enunciate our principles to the people."

Frustrated by the debacle of Goldwater's campaign and credibility in 1964, Rubel and Co. looked for a fresh approach. Said Salvatori: "When I saw Ronnie on television, I knew he was our boy!"

Said Tuttle: "After we took that terrible defeat in 1964, we knew we had to do something....We believed in the free enterprise system.

We felt that if it was going to be preserved, instead of going around bellyaching about it, we should go out and do something about it.

We gathered people around who had a common interest and decided to help Ron."

Strange coincidence — the people with "a common interest" in Ron's candidacy were all millionaires...

The inner circle of Reagan's "Friends" was completed with the addition of the following people: Leonard Firestone, president of the Firestone Tire and Rubber Company; Leland M. Kaiser, multimillionaire former Board Chairman of Insurance Securities, Inc.; wealthy San Francisco industrialists Jaquelin Hume and Arch Monson, Jr. (of Basic Vegetables and Autocall, respectively); Taft Schreiber, vice president of MCA, Inc., parent company of Universal Pictures, Universal Studios, and Decca Records; Edward Mills, vice president of Holmes Tuttle Enterprises; and William French Smith, partner in the Los Angeles law firm of Gibson, Dunn and Crutcher. A year later, in 1966, Justin Dart — president of Rexall Drugs — joined former CIA chief John R. McCloy among new entrants to the Reagan inner circle.

"Everyone of them is a self-made man," said Holmes Tuttle about the original millionaire backers. Together, they helped make Ronald Reagan what he is today.

Very early, the millionaire backers foresaw the prospect of becoming a White House Kitchen Cabinet.

"It didn't take a real smart man to know that we had a viable candidate for Governor, and if he did a good job he would be presidential timber."

A political public relations firm was employed to promote Reagan: Spencer-Roberts—"the best," according to Holmes Tuttle; an ideologically pure firm that will not serve Democrats.

Once in the Governor's Office in Sacramento, Reagan solicited recommendations from his millionaire backers for "thirty-five or forty of the top jobs..." "He didn't have to accept our recommendations, but I'll say this, in all but one or two cases he did." (Tuttle)

Though the millionaire backers remained active, they shunned official positions. Still, virtually everyone appointed to an official position was an employer or an executive. Reagan was candid: "My administration makes no bones about being business-oriented."

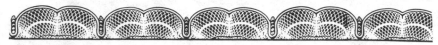

Meanwhile, Henry Salvatori coordinated Reagan's 1968 foray into Presidential politics. "By early 1968 Salvatori had assembled a smoothly running Presidential machine..."

All told, the millionaire backers raised $366,557 for Reagan's 1968 campaign. $72,500 was raised for the communications network alone at the Miami Beach convention. This proved to be an expensive lesson in big-time politics — but one which finally paid dividends to the millionaire backers in 1980.

Emulating Dale as well as Andrew Carnegie, Reagan won friends and influenced people—i.e., businessmen—while in Sacramento. Verne Orr, Reagan's finance director, disarmingly concedes Reagan's bias:

"It is natural that the type of special interest group that puts you there [in office] is the one that you're going to listen to more closely. In our case it was the conservative groups, the business groups, that put this administration in. They are our constituency."

New faces from this constituency joined the Reagan team in the years leading up to 1980. When, after the 1980 election, Reagan formed a "transition team" to identify potential appointees, Kitchen Cabinet members were prominently represented.

Justin Dart

Headed by William French Smith, an 18-member team included the late Justin Dart (who had become perhaps the most influential millionaire backer); Holmes Tuttle; Henry Salvatori; the late Alfred Bloomingdale, president of Diners Club; Earl M. Jorgensen, president of Jorgensen Steel Company; Theodore Cummings, a steel and aluminum magnate; Caspar Weinberger of Bechtel; Chicago businessman Daniel Terra; Senator Paul Laxalt; Edwin Meese III; Charles Z. Wick; and four others.

Reagan's mandate to the appointments team was to attract "some of the big names in business — men who make $100,000 a year." This was an assignment Kitchen Cabinet members were eminently suited to fulfill. Their great success sprang, in part, from self-nominations.

As usual, top Kitchen Cabinet members stayed aloof from official positions. Justin Dart expressed a characteristic sentiment, saying:

"I could have probably had pretty much whatever I wanted, but I thought I could do more good this way [as a private Reagan adviser] than by calling up the secretary of state everyday to ask when I could go to the toilet."

FOR YOUR KITCHEN CABINET

Preoccupied with the 1980 merger which produced Dart-Kraft Inc. — the 27th largest industrial firm in the U.S. — Dart accepted only a minor directorship with the Communications Satellite Corporation. (Dart's estate is immense: after making his first million selling "medicinal whiskey" during Prohibition, Dart accumulated between $20 and $200 million.)

Though Holmes Tuttle also stayed out of the limelight, his son, Robert became a special presidential assistant, and his daughter-in-law, Donna, became a $70,000-a-year commerce undersecretary for travel and tourism.

High appointments were common, however, among junior members of the Kitchen Cabinet.

William French Smith became Attorney-General. Edwin Meese became presidential counselor, and (at this writing) Attorney-General designate. Caspar Weinberger became Defense Secretary. Charles Wick became U.S. Information Agency chief. Paul Laxalt became chairman of the Republican Party. And William Wilson became Vatican Ambassador.

For a while, Wilson also ran an "Office of the Kitchen Cabinet" in the Old Executive Office Building across from the West Wing of the White House.

Concurrently, several millionare backers set up permanent quarters in Washington — Dart, Jorgensen, Bloomingdale. With help from their friends, the Reagans reintroduced high fashion to Washington.

Society reporters eagerly recounted Nancy Reagan's $822,000 plan to refurbish White House living quarters, and a $209,000 gift of gilt-edged china.

Still, Nancy regally dismissed a postcard depicting her as Queen Nancy; quote:

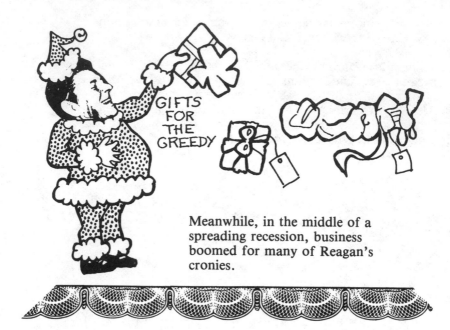

GIFTS
FOR
THE
GREEDY

Meanwhile, in the middle of a spreading recession, business boomed for many of Reagan's cronies.

Henry Salvatori crowed that "business hasn't been this good in my lifetime." Dart-Kraft reported a 47 percent gain in after-tax income during the first nine months of 1981. And Jorgensen Steel felt no pain: "We know the recession is out there," said Earl Jorgensen, "but so far we have been fortunate not to have been affected at all."

Reagan was so good to business, in fact, and vice versa, that Reagan's hard-won image as a friend of the people began to slip away.

In February, 1981, only 23 percent of the public felt that Reagan favored the wealthy; by September, this percentage had more than doubled — rising to 52 percent. Apparently, giving the jet set *carte blanche* in Washington had proven a bit rich for the public's blood. The fat-cat image began to reappear...

This has always been a vulnerable point in Reagan's propaganda armor. Another key weakness is Reagan's affinity for the ultra-right. Camouflaged better, by Reagan, than by any other spokesman for the right, Reagan's views are nevertheless extreme.

The Far-Right Stuff

Polls consistently show that Ronald Reagan appears less reactionary to his audience than his words and deeds seem in cold print. His warm, scolding, Sunday-school-manner contradicts the message of his program and speeches: "He doesn't look like a mad bomber," says Hedrick Smith.

Frederick Dutton, a former Edmund Brown advisor and long-time power broker, commented in 1981 that "Reagan is underestimated. We tried to make him out a sinister figure, as Jimmy Carter did in 1980. It didn't work. Reagan has no harsh edge, he's terribly pleasant. People like him, and we didn't understand that."

Not everyone likes Reagan, by any means — but most voters have fallen for him most of the time for 20 years.

Underneath the facade, however, there beats the heart of a genuine far-rightist. Though Reagan loves to reminisce about his "liberal" post-war days, these days were short and wintry, to say the least. SAG President Reagan quickly emerged as a leading Hollywood anti-Communist. He supported Democrat Harry Truman in 1948 only because Truman had distinguished himself by immaculate anti-Communism.

In 1952 Reagan supported Republican Dwight D. Eisenhower.

The 1950's were halcyon years for Ronald Reagan. Encouraged by *GE*, Reagan shifted from Cold War liberalism to industrial-strength rightism. The versatile actor thus found a path to public influence in a time of stormy reaction.

With McCarthyite anti-Communism in its glory, Reagan became a McCarthyite *par excellence*. After Senator McCarthy's death in the late 50's, was well positioned to assume his mantle. After Goldwater's defeat, Reagan's claim to far-right leadership was rarely disputed.

To this day Reagan retains a lingering fondness for McCarthyism. On the radio in 1979, Reagan made the following remark:

It's true the Senator used a shotgun when a rifle was needed, injuring the innocent along with the guilty. Nevertheless, his broadsides should not be used today to infer that all who opposed Communist subversion were hysterical zealots.

A more personal, less guarded statement came at a presidential dinner, when hard-right counselor Meese toasted McCarthy as a great senator. Reagan turned to say,

"Isn't it a shame what happened to McCarthy and Roy?"

(Roy Cohn was McCarthy's assistant.)

Reagan's record as a zealous anti-Communist goes back even to his ostensibly left-leaning phase in the 1940's. As early as 1947, when he returned to Eureka College to crown the Pumpkin Festival queen, Reagan was awarded an honorary doctorate for "understanding and exposing Communists and their influence as president of the Screen Actors Guild."

That same year he lectured Hedda Hopper on the Red Menace. When 500 Hollywood directors and actors protested the 1947 efforts of the House Unamerican Activities Committee (HUAC) to punish unpopular views, Reagan's name was conspicuously absent from the list.

The next year Reagan testified before HUAC.

According to the *New York Times*, when Reagan entered the HUAC chambers...

"there was a long drawn-out 'ooooh' from the jam-packed, predominantly female audience."

WITCH HUNT

The star proved to be a friendly witness, with no qualms about blacklisting Hollywood radicals.

Shortly afterwards, ten writers and directors were banned. The Inquisition had begun. Ronald Reagan approved.

GROPPER-

Reagan's McCarthyite career was off to an auspicious start. Though he may have felt that he lacked a developed worldview, there was no doubt about his animosity to Communism and the Soviet Union.

Reagan condemned ''the class warfare boys'' — ''the little Red brothers'' — at every opportunity. He saw U.S. free enterprise endangered:

> ''Free now of the Nazi wolf at their throat, the Communists gathered themselves to turn against the U.S. as the citadel of capitalism.''

In January, 1951, Reagan wrote that Communists are ''traitors practicing treason.'' This missed the point. The McCarthyite inquisition in the early fifties was only peripherally concerned with national security. At stake, in reality, were human-rights issues: the right to employment without political discrimination; the right to free speech without penalty. SAG and its president came down squarely in opposition to these rights.

Typical of the cogent arguments offered by Hollywood anti-Communists was Gary Cooper's H.U.A.C. testimony in favor of banning the Communist party:

''Although I have never read Karl Marx and don't know the basis of communism beyond what I have picked up from hearsay, from what I hear I don't like it because it isn't on the level.''

Take my word for it!

In 1951, the SAG directors declared that "All participants in the international Communist conspiracy against our nation should be exposed for what they are — enemies of our country." SAG also gave tacit consent to the industry blacklist of dissidents, voting to require all SAG members to sign non-Communist affidavits (thus clearly signaling its willingness to shunt aside actors opposed to political hiring and firing.)

Though described by Nancy as "a leader in the industry drive against Communists and their sympathizers," Reagan was still, at this juncture, no more than a neophyte conservative. Clearly a right-wing Democrat, Reagan was not yet an extremist. That came next.

As *GE* spokesman, Reagan took on the protective coloring of corporate ideology. His speeches nosedived far to the right. When the idea of his televised 1964 pro-Goldwater speech was proposed, Goldwater showed some reluctance, fearing that Reagan might say something imprudent. Reagan reassured him:

THERE ISN'T ONE KOOKY THING IN THE SPEECH. IT'S THE SAME ONE I'VE BEEN GIVING UP AND DOWN THE COUNTRY FOR YEARS!

What did Reagan say in this speech?

On foreign affairs. "We are at war with the most dangerous enemy ever known" — Communism..."We are asked to buy our safety from the threat of the Bomb by selling into permanent slavery our fellow human beings enslaved behind the Iron Curtain." U.S. foreign aid "finances socialism all over the world...Some of our foreign aid funds provide extra wives for Kenya government officials."

On domestic affairs. "The greatest good for the greatest number is a high-sounding phrase but contrary to the very basis of our Nation, unless it is accompanied by recognition that we have certain rights which cannot be infringed upon." "We have a tax rate that takes from the private sector a percentage of income greater than any civilized nation has ever survived."

"Lowell Mason has written 'American business is being harassed, bled, even black jacked under a preposterous crazy quilt system of laws'." "Under Urban Renewal, the assault on freedom carries on. Private property rights have become so diluted that public interest is anything a few planners decide it should be."

"Have we the courage and the will to face up to the immorality and discrimination of the progressive surtax, and demand a return to traditional proportionate taxation?... Sumner Slichter has said, 'If a visitor from Mars looked at our tax policy, he would conclude it had been designed by a Communist spy to make free enterprise unworkable.'"

"The doctor's fight against socialized medicine is your fight."

Reagan also deplored the United Nations, questioned the wisdom of Social Security policies, and criticized welfare in his usual anecdotal way.

71

Once in early 1980 Reagan was asked if he could think of any issue debated by Barry Goldwater and Ted Kennedy on which he would support Kennedy. Reagan paused, smiled, finally responded,

"I think it would be very, very difficult."

Similarly, in 1974, Reagan reaffirmed his Goldwaterite orthodoxy:

"My beliefs now are the beliefs I held when I first ran for office, when I campaigned for Barry Goldwater in '64..."

This particular leopard does not change his spots...

Since Reagan emerged from Goldwater's shadow, it is worth remembering what Goldwater stood for.

In 1962 Goldwater published a programmatic book called *Why Not Victory?* Victory over what? Chapter 1 offers a clear answer: "The World-Wide Communist Menace."

Stirring martial rhetoric echoes on every page. Goldwater's main point, reiterated constantly, is that: "We are at war; not a cold war but a real war — we can call it the Communist War, war of a more deadly nature than any we have fought before... a death stuggle with an enemy which is waging a new kind of total war...We may well be now engaged in a phase of World War III..."

"Russia is the aggressor nation determined to conquer the world; peace for Russia means defeat for the United States..."

"We are *against* disarmament. We are against it because we *need* our armaments — all we presently have and more. We need weapons for both limited and unlimited war...My opponents adroitly try to make it appear that I am in favor of nuclear war, that I would make war the prime instrument of our policy. I can't imagine what makes them think that...

Our job, first and foremost, is to persuade the enemy that we would rather follow the world to Kingdom Come than consign it to Hell under communism...We will never reconcile ourselves to the Communists' possession of power of any kind in any part of the world..."

What did Goldwater's defense of the free-world entail? Very little freedom:

"Freedom, in the sense of self-determination, is a worthy objective, but if granting self-determination to the Algerian rebels entails sweeping that area into the Sino-Soviet orbit, then Algerian freedom must be postponed. Justice is a worthy objective, but if justice for Bantus entails driving the government of the Union of South Africa away from the West, then the Bantus must be prepared to carry their identification cards yet a while longer. Prosperity is a worthy objective, but if providing higher living standards gets in the way of producing sufficient weapons to be able to resist possible Communist aggression, then material sacrifices will have to be made."

This is admirably clear.

Consistently, Goldwater urged "whatever action is needed to dislodge communism from the front yard of the Western Hemisphere" — Cuba — and described the 1954 CIA overthrow of a left-leaning Guatemalan goverment as "our single full-fledged triumph...We served our national interests, and, in so doing, we saved the Guatemalan people the ultimate misery."

At home, "We must avoid economic collapse by scaling down extravagant and useless domestic programs, and the squandering of our money on unrealistic world-wide aid programs."

Reagan never faulted Goldwater's views, but he did feel that Goldwater's tactics left something to be desired. Voters were not calmed when the Senator from Arizona suggested, on the campaign trail, that it might be useful to "lob one into the men's room of the Kremlin." Fear of war played a large part in the huge anti-Goldwater vote in 1964. Enter Reagan.

"People criticize Ronnie for having no political experience. But he has a great image. Look at the Goldwater experience. His philosophy was sound, but he didn't articulate it moderately.

"Reagan has a similar philosophy, but he can express his thought." Salvatori

From the debacle of Goldwater's campaign Reagan learned a vital lesson: *Never sound like an extremist.* Writing in the far-right *National Review,* Reagan summarized the 1964 Republican failure — Goldwater had allowed himself to be seen "as advancing a kind of radical departure from the status quo." How to rectify this?

"In short — time now for the soft sell to prove our radicalism was an illusion."

This sales judgement put Reagan in harmony with the ad men hired to fine-tune his image, Spencer-Roberts and BASICO.

Initially, Bill Roberts felt some misgivings:

> "We had reservations about Reagan. We had heard that Reagan was a real right-winger and we thought that a right-wing kind of candidacy would not be a successful one."

But Reagan proved flexible, authorizing Roberts to quarantine him from extremist supporters:

> "Any people we knew who were Birchers or were real Birch sympathizers or even strongly conservative, we deliberately excluded from positions in the campaign."

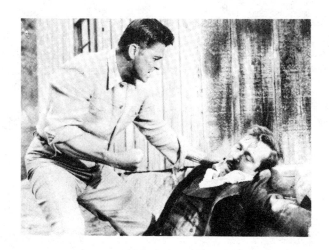

Not that Spencer and Roberts were politically moderate — on the contrary, like Reagan, they had worked in 1962 to keep the national John Birch Society PR director John Rousselot in Congress after his Birch membership won him negative publicity. But this time Spencer and Roberts were aiming for the governor's office, and they didn't want to misfire.

As it turned out, though, Rousselot, the Birch Society, and rightism *did* become a campaign problem, thanks to Reagan's indiscretion. At a Republican gathering Reagan unwisely enthused that...

"Johnny Rousselot is a terrific fellow. He called Stu Spencer and offered all his help in the campaign. In fact, he said he would do anything from calling me names in public to endorsement — whatever we want."

Whatever would serve Reagan best, the Birch Society's PR director would do. Rousselot later became a Reagan congressional liaison and Western states coordinator for the 1984 Reagan for President campaign.

Though publicity about his Rousselot remarks injured Reagan, he nevertheless refrained from repudiating the Birchers (or, for that matter, the Minutemen or the Soldiers of the Cross, who also praised Reagan).

Nixon had scorned the far-right in 1962, and had demoralized many followers. Reagan wanted to eat his cake, too. (In 1980, Reagan repudiated a Ku Klux Klan endorsement.)

BASICO also worked to camouflage Reagan's militant outlook:

"We made certain that Reagan came across as a reasonable guy, not as a fanatic. One of the first things I got Ron to do was to stop using that terrible phrase, 'totalitarian ant heap.' It just sounded too harsh. His basic speech was too negative, so we provided him with creative alternatives to combat that Far Right image."

Also helpful at this stage was the right-wing radio pastor W.S. McBirnie. Said Reagan:

"We discussed the putting over or you might say the selling of this philosophy...Dr. McBirnie came up with the phrase 'Creative Society.' Some people objected to it because they said it sounded too much like the term 'Great Society' — which, incidentally, was first mentioned by Karl Marx — but I favored it because I said it was an alternative to the Great Society."

The reason for all this caution? Said Roberts:

NEWSWEEK, JUNE 7, 1965

"Reagan is very new in politics, but he's a hot product. He's hot now because he's kind of supplanted Goldwater in people's minds. But we're going to shift that image. In fact, we've got to if we're going to win."

And so they did. Still, the basic outlines of Reagan's views were clear to the discerning. Barry Goldwater extended approval: "I have always looked on Ronald Reagan as one of the leaders of the conservative movement in this country, and I would say that, if he continues in his successful political career, I don't think you could deny that he would be the leader. And I would very, very gladly serve with him, under him or alongside him."

And this, too, has come to pass.

After three years as president very little has happened to suggest that Ronald Reagan is any less right-wing now than ever. Though he has shown a talent for bending with the wind, Reagan reasserts his ultra-conservative leanings whenever the opportunity arises. Beneath the smiling celluloid exterior we find an angry ideologue — "the most overtly ideological President in the nation's history," says chronicler Laurence Barrett of *Time.*

In 1976, *National Review* publisher William Rusher toyed with the idea of an "Independence" party, intended — in the words of Reagan's U.N. representative, Jeane Kirkpatrick — to "include the 'populist' followers of George Wallace and the 'conservative' Republicans."

Eight years later Rusher pronounced himself entirely satisfied with the present Republican leadership: "Genuine conservatives are by and large overjoyed by Reagan and rightly so."

Anti-feminist crusader Phyllis Schafly, long an ardent right-winger — the author of a 1964 pro-Goldwater tract — summarized her view of Reagan's first term by calling Reagan "a wonderful man with all the right instincts." When the ERA fell short of passage, "Schafly praised the Holy Lord and Ronald Reagan."

Like a thundering herd of elephants, Reagan's far-right program tramples everything in its path. It *matters*. For poor and working people, here and abroad, Reagan's program has spelled danger, injury, and insult.

Nemesis In The White House

Test your knowledge — see if you can identify the president profiled below...

With practiced charm, this president rose to power on the wings of big business support. He campaigned for the White House as "an outsider." Characterized by the *Wall Street Journal* as "a foe of Washington's big government," he proclaimed the Federal government to be "a horrible, bureaucratic mess."

"It is disorganized, wasteful, has no purpose, and its policies — when they exist — are incomprehensible or devised by special interest groups with little regard for the welfare of the average American citizen."

WHO IS THAT MASKED PRESIDENT, MOMMY?

Cold to the public sector, this president radiates warmth for business. He campaigned as "a firm advocate of the private enterprise system," vehemently opposed to the "rigid, bureaucratic, centralized planning you get in Communist countries."

The *Wall Street Journal* smiled that he "sings the praises" of finance and industry.

Opposed to New Deal politics, this president campaigned for fiscal conservatism.

He indicted the U.S. tax system as a bloated "disgrace to the human race," urged the severance of payments to 1.3 million welfare recipients, and called mandatory school desegregation by means of busing "the most serious threat to education I can remember."

With glowing faith he extolled the family, work, patriotism, and religion.

Does all this sound familiar?

Our mystery president — we'll call him X — proved to be a devoted friend of big business. Pre-appointment, his 11 cabinet officers *averaged* a yearly income of $211,000. Overall, his administration took many decisive pro-business steps:

1. Aided by the Business Roundtable, X formulated tax cuts which dropped the effective corporate tax rate to 13%. Eighty-five percent of his tax breaks accrued to the upper half of the income scale. Ninety percent of a capital gains tax cut benefited the *top 1%* of the nation. And builders of new factories were rewarded with an investment tax credit — whether they created new jobs or not.

As X told the Business Council, "We evolved the tax proposal in a way that I think you would have had you been in office."

2. Arguing in favor of "less burdensome" environmental and safety regulations, X deregulated natural gas and eliminated crude oil price controls. Thanks to decontrol, the energy industry stood to gain $57 billion over six years, while paying only $7 billion in new windfall profits taxes. (Figures courtesy of the government.)

Also lifted were regulations in the fields of air, rail, and truck transport; communications; and finance.

3. Not surprisingly, profits soared. Citibank reported "the highest return on equity in the more than fifty years Citibank has compiled these figures." *Business Week* reported that U.S. firms were sitting pretty — "atop a record $80 billion pile of cash."

X's stated goal had been to stimulate investment and production. What happened, instead, was that productivity fell, while a new merger movement (one colossus buying another) subsituted for new investment.

Said the *New York Times:* "No president in living memory has courted big business as ardently..."

Does *your* living memory begin to recall this mystery president?

Consider the following: President X proved himself ready to decertify striking Federal unions, while supporting all business anti-unionism. He increased both deficits and defense spending while cutting back on domestic spending. (A total of $27.6 billion in projected domestic cuts included reductions in job training, Social Security, and other programs.)

X sparked a planned recession. After appointing a majority of the seven-member Federal Reserve Board — including chairman Paul A. Volcker — he encouraged the Fed to strictly limit the money supply. His vice-president told the Business Council that there is "no higher priority than controlling inflation." (Inflation hurts business by making exports costlier and hence less saleable).

Chairman Paul Volcker

83

Economic Digression...

Basically, the Federal Reserve Board expands or contracts the national money supply. A policy of contraction ("tight money") limits borrowing, since less total money is on hand. When less money circulates, the price of money rises (i.e., the interest rate), and spending falls, both by individuals (consumption and by firms (investment). When investment falls, employment falls.

The purpose of a tight money policy is to lower prices. This works if sellers cut prices to compete for the reduced money in circulation.

For business, disinflation lowers the price of products sold domestically, but ups the volume of export sales. For the public, disinflation lowers some prices, raises the cost of imports, and ups joblessness (i.e., recession). [End digression]

Encouraged by X, Volcker's Fed triggered a serious recession. For the first time since 1933 the Fed raised its discount rate by a full point. The prime rate skyrocketed, productivity fell, unemployment rose steeply, and a two-year fall in real median incomes ensued.

ME? TIGHT?

WITH MONEY HARD TO GET ITS PRICE GOES UP YOU BET! THE FEWER THE DOLLARS THE TIGHTER THE COLLARS FOR CONSUMERS AND WORKERS AND DEBTS!

It became clear, however, that X's recessionary policy harbored dangerous new inflationary impulses: both Federal deficits and defense spending rose.

The rationale for heightened war production was X's accusation that the USSR had carried out a military build-up "excessive far beyond any legitimate requirements."

Always an unyielding supporter of the Vietnam war, X initiated stern economic sanctions against Vietnam, the USSR, etc.

His foreign policy was guided by a National Security Adviser self-described as "a hawk," who (said the *NY Times)* sees everything "in terms of the rivalry of the Soviet Union and the U.S."

X persuaded NATO governments to emplace nuclear weapons aimed at the USSR, and to increase military spending 3% per year (after inflation) for five years. Meanwhile, the U.S. embarked on 5% yearly military increases — projected, over three years, to increase total war spending by $60 billion.

X urged Japanese rearmament, and envisioned "rolling back" Soviet power in East Europe. Confronted by revolution in Central America, he initiated *Operation Libertad* (aimed at Cuba) and sent scores of military "advisors" to prop up the tyrannical, failing government of El Salvador.

According to his National Security Advisor, "The U.S. will never permit a new Nicaragua, even if it must take the most reprehensible measures to prevent it."

All this reflected a drive to assure U.S. military supremacy. Militarism flowered. Nuclear weapons were produced at accelerating rates. Virtually every weapon the Pentagon proposed was pegged for production. A special force was readied for lightning raids to global trouble spots.

In Western Europe, a drive was launched to improve non-nuclear U.S. forces. X explicitly discussed ''limited nuclear war'' outside U.S. borders. Revived civil defense plans went to Congress, and a renewed commitment to military conscription was urged. Finally, U.S. arms shipments worth many billions of dollars went to the world's ten leading violators of human rights (including Zaire, Chile, and the Phillippines), while U.S. arms sales nearly doubled overall.

Though X was never universally loved, he did fare well in many polls. Successfully downplaying his early politics (e.g., 1960's praise for segregationist George Wallace), X was voted into the White House by 28% of the eligible public. (Just 54% of the electorate voted.)

At first quite popular, X's public rating fell until the approach of the next election, when he recorded a 29% jump in public approval (from 32% to 61%).

THE PROBLEM WITH POLITICAL JOKES IS THAT THEY GET ELECTED!

Running for re-election, X cast himself as the outsider, still at odds with the bureaucracy. His pollster had advised this, saying: "It is crucial that President X keep the image that he is not part of the traditional political establishment."

Ready to cast your ballots? The time has come. X — the mystery president — the masked man in the White House — is none other than...

James Earl Carter!

Any resemblance between Carter's record and Reagan's...is not coincidental. Despite their best efforts to pose as night and day, Carter and Reagan are in fact surprisingly alike.

The surprise element in the Carter/Reagan equation stems from the fact that Carter and Reagan conjure up highly opposed images. Where Reagan is unabashedly warlike, Carter seems to be a man of peace, ready to turn the other cheek. Where Reagan talks military "greatness," Carter talks "human rights."

Fervently, Reagan castigates Carter for spendthrift ways; by contrast, Reagan poses as prudently tight-fisted, the sort of man who would pinch a penny until it bled...

While Reagan slams every form of "evil Communism," Carter tilted against Russia but befriended China...

These differences are very real. Nevertheless, their importance has been greatly overrated by most commentators. Apples and oranges differ, too. Like all recent presidents, Carter and Reagan are effectively warlike and pro-business. But unlike Nixon, Kennedy *et.al.,* Jimmy and Ronnie share something new and unique — a post-liberal strategy. Though this strategy permits tactical differences, it is otherwise unitary.

To fully grasp the Carter/Reagan strategy requires a brief detour through recent history...

The Warfare/Welfare State

Starting in 1933 the U.S. embarked on a vital new political course (largely uncontested until 1976-1984). The hallmark of this 45-year period was a special strategy for attracting power and profits — popularly called "liberalism."

20th century liberalism promoted worldwide U.S. power by means of a double commitment to government spending: for warfare ("defense") and welfare.

In the 19th century, "liberalism" had denoted a government policy of *laissez faire* (non-interference in business); in the special conditions of Roosevelt's U.S., however, the term acquired a diametrically opposed meaning.

Consider the situation. The 1930's were a period of unprecedented global depression and militarism. The U.S. was mired in a spate of business failures and jeopardized by the rise of expansionist German and Japanese regimes. A solution was needed.

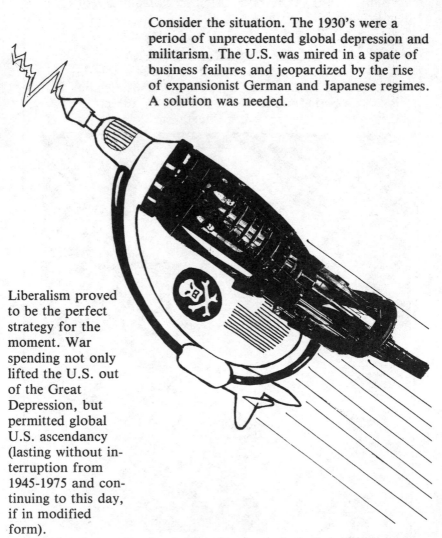

Liberalism proved to be the perfect strategy for the moment. War spending not only lifted the U.S. out of the Great Depression, but permitted global U.S. ascendancy (lasting without interruption from 1945-1975 and continuing to this day, if in modified form).

U.S. business gained immensely from military ascendancy: the foreign investment climate vastly improved; war spending created a giant permanent market for industry — and a giant borrower for banks; and U.S. labor grew more pliant as its share of the expanding pie grew larger.

Add domestic spending — to limit unemployment and shield the unemployed — and the liberal equation is complete.

"Aggregate demand" for U.S. business products rose both domestically and globally. Profits, employment, and wages went up.

With a stake in the overall warfare/welfare strategy, working people became the basis for the fabled "Roosevelt coalition" which made liberalism electorally viable.

Initially, the demand for public spending came from business. An early step had been the formation of the Federal Reserve System in 1913. Financial markets had seemed perilously unstable and bankers hoped that Federal regulation could limit monetary anarchy.

The 1929 stock market crash proved the need for much sterner measures. Elite financiers promptly demanded government help to reduce "uneconomic competition." The Chamber of Commerce and the National Association of Manufacturers chimed in with similar requests in 1931.

President Hoover initially resisted an active Federal role in the reconstruction of the economy. He had a somewhat unusual explanation for the collapse...

In the summer of 1932, however, Hoover relented and the Reconstruction Finance Corporation was formed (to loan public funds to private business).

After Franklin Roosevelt's 1933 inauguration a wave of new programs began. First came the National Industrial Recovery Act, authorizing price and product regulation by industry representatives.

In 1935, the Social Security Act was passed — mandating social security retirement pensions, unemployment insurance, and funds for dependent children, the blind, and poor elders ineligible for pensions.

About the same time, public work projects set a precedent for direct Federal action to reduce unemployment.

In 1951, under Truman, welfare aid was granted to the permanently and totally disabled.

Finally, under Kennedy/Johnson and Nixon, welfare eligibility rules were relaxed, Medicare and Medicaid were funded, the food stamp program started, and various housing, disability, and job training programs got underway.

This was the welfare half of the equation.

Meanwhile, warfare was not neglected. Spurred, in part, by wars in Korea and Vietnam, military spending rose at an amazing rate — so fast that even General Dwight D. Eisenhower issued a memorable warning about the power of the "military-industrial complex."

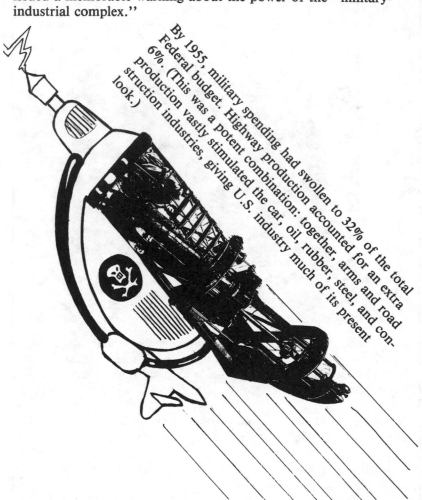

By 1955, military spending had swollen to 32% of the total Federal budget. Highway production accounted for an extra 6%. (This was a potent combination: together, arms and road production vastly stimulated the car, oil, rubber, steel, and construction industries, giving U.S. industry much of its present look.)

Though war spending fell as a percentage of the 1960's budget, it continued to grow in absolute terms.

Thus was born "the affluent society" — not in spite of liberalism, but thanks to it.

In other words, for half a century public spending has been a massive and unmistakable fact of contemporary life. Neither side of the usual debate between "liberals" and "conservatives" calls for *an end* to public spending. Generally, liberals push for relative parity between guns and butter, while conservatives emphasize a "mostly-guns" approach.

In this spectrum of debate, most presidents since Roosevelt have hewed essentially to the liberal strategy, however reluctantly. Though Eisenhower, for example, did not stress welfare, he did not actually reverse the welfare trend. That was left for Carter — with Reagan hot on his heels. And not even Reagan has yet succeeded in undermining the *relative* parity of war and social spending — though this is clearly his goal.

Essentially, the curve of liberalism since 1933 looks like this...

- Roosevelt (until 1945) —— BIG JUMP
- Truman (until 1952) —— MODEST JUMP
- Eisenhower (until 1960) —— STANDING AT ATTENTION
- Kennedy (until 1963) —— MODEST JUMP
- Johnson (until 1968) —— GREAT LEAP FORWARD
- Nixon (until 1975) —— MODEST JUMP
- Ford (until 1976) —— ASLEEP
- Carter (until 1980) —— MODEST REVERSAL
- Reagan (until   ) —— BIG REVERSAL

The Inflation Party

The success of the liberal strategy sprang in large part from the longevity of the famous Roosevelt coalition. Far-sighted business, unionized labor, and elements of the poor coalesced into an effective voting bloc. Though as early as 1938 "Dixiecrats" (conservative southern Democrats) allied themselves with northern Republicans to oppose the new liberal majority, they had little luck for several decades.

The basic direction of the warfare/welfare state is set by business, thanks to the power of business money; still, labor and the poor have typically won enough concessions to remain loyal. In the late-1940's for example, industry-wide productivity agreements guaranteed unionized labor a share of the revenues arising from enhanced productivity. And productivity rose steadily...

Though the Roosevelt coalition weakened in the 1950's, it retained its grip on public policy. When Dwight Eisenhower made serious inroads into the Democratic electorate — winning 374 northern counties that Roosevelt and Truman had previously held five times in a row — it seemed possible that a change was at hand.

Eisenhower, however, was a middle-of-the-road politician who had been courted for the presidency *by both parties* before embracing Republicanism. Not until 1964 did a genuine right-wing challenge emerge — when Barry Goldwater carried the fallen McCarthy's torch to the White House steps.

In some ways, conditions in 1964 were ripe for a right-wing victory. Liberalism has an inherent economic contradiction — that it promotes inflation in lieu of unemployment. (Public spending lifts not only productivity and employment, but also prices.) Rising prices do not jeopardize the liberal coalition when the public worries more about unemployment than about inflation. *But the very success of the liberal bloc produces heightened inflation fears.*

As early as 1952 political scientist Samuel Lubell felt that the Democratic constituency had won enough prosperity to fear the erosion of its gains through inflation:

"No new governmental benefits could be pressed for any of the Democratic voting elements without threatening to take something away from other Democratic voters."

In brief, class differences tend to tear the liberal bloc apart. The once-poor find that the aid needs of the still-poor contribute to high taxes and prices. Yesterday's ragged CIO worker who now owns a home may not want to share prosperity with today's frail elders or unemployed single mothers with dependent children.

If you no longer fear unemployment, it is highly rational to favor reduced public spending.

This, to a certain degree, is the conventional Republican prescription: Chill the economic fever with a recessionary ice-pack. Hence the appeal of Republicanism. But, until recently, most Republicans resisted the impulse to carry this view to an extreme. They may have wanted *less* spending — i.e., less employment and inflation — but within limits.

In corporate society, "the goal of economic policy," says Frank Ackerman, is "to find and maintain the perfect amount of unemployment." Democrats usually prefer a few less percentage points of joblessness than Republicans do.

However, in unstable times, preferences change. Newly affluent Democrats often go Republican when inflationary winds blow, then turn Democrat again when jobs are gusted away.

By 1964, enough pent-up fear of inflation had accumulated to permit a true conservative challenge to the liberal majority. Several factors, however, prevented a 1964 conservative victory: persisting prosperity, most dramatically proven by the success of an $11 billion tax cut; the addition of new elements to the old liberal coalition (elders and Blacks); and Barry Goldwater's buccaneering style.

Reagan later told reporters that "Barry *proved* you can't run against Social Security."

Johnson, promising Medicare, gave elders "a stake in an inflation they had lost hope of halting..." (Lubell).

And Goldwater frightened millions with rash saber-rattling...

So inept was Goldwater's challenge to liberalism that the liberal bloc gathered considerable new strength.

In seven elections since Roosevelt, Democratic presidential candidates had been able to win just one county Roosevelt had not won. Johnson won 133 counties and 460 New England towns that Roosevelt had never captured. Democrats also won 46 extra seats in Congress, disrupting the Republican/Dixiecrat bloc.

The time seemed ripe for an even Newer Deal — which Johnson obligingly furnished in the form of "the Great Society." Mixing the war in Indochina with redoubled welfare, Johnson's Great Society offered even more guns and butter than the Rooseveltian original.

AND HERRE'S RONNNIE!

Nevertheless, despite Goldwater's smashing defeat, Lubell commented at the time that "the final act of this drama has still to be fought out." Act II and screenstar Ronald Reagan were waiting in the wings...

Richard Milhous Nixon is a central figure in the crisis of liberalism, since many Rooseveltian contradictions crystallized during Nixon's tenure in office.

Few people would casually call Nixon a liberal. In time-honored Republican style Nixon staged two recessions. (Eisenhower had prompted three.) Meanwhile, Nixon's McCarthyite mania for FBI skullduggery is legend. Still, there was a definite liberal side to Nixon's administration. Under Nixon, Medicaid expanded, food stamps were liberalized, Social Security payments accelerated, and the Comprehensive Employment and Training Act passed. Though Nixon was a seasoned anti-Communist, he defied his Russophobe instincts to pioneer detente.

What went wrong during Nixon's semi-liberal administration? From the standpoint of business, almost everything.

Starting in 1969-70, the Vietnam inflation turned into a strange and disturbing phenomenon, "stagflation" — with both prices *and* joblessness rising. (There had been nearly 15 years of comparatively stable prices before Johnson floated $20 billion in unsupported paper bonds to support the Vietnam War.)

In 1971, partly as a result of the Vietnam inflation, the Bretton Woods world monetary agreement collapsed. This was a major blow both to the stability of world money markets and to the dominant position of the dollar.

Also in 1971, the U.S. recorded its first trade deficit of the century (more imports than exports).

In 1973, the OPEC price coup jolted inflation upwards. Now, the oil-producing countries were dictating to Western powers.

Earlier, in 1953, when an Iranian government had nationalized U.S. oil companies, the CIA had engineered its overthrow. In 1973, however, the U.S. was shipwrecked in Vietnam and Cambodia. Less eager to police the high seas, the U.S. passively watched as the price of oil rose from roughly $2 a barrel to more than $8. (In 1981, this price was $36.)

All oil-dependent industries were hit: airlines, petrochemicals, auto companies, agribusiness, etc.

To make matters worse, steeper recessions now yielded smaller cuts in inflation. (This is another way of defining stagflation.)

From 1966 to 1980, yearly inflation averaged 8%, four times the 1947 to 1966 rate. A series of recessions did little to abate rising prices.

The crowning blow to liberalism came in 1975 — the loss of Indochina. This spelled an end to unambiguous U.S. supremacy in world politics. The aura of U.S. invincibility dissolved.

Meanwhile, wages and welfare rose to historic highs in 1972-74. The link between the two is that welfare limits competition for jobs, thus keeping wages higher than they might otherwise be. (If more people compete for the same number of jobs, wage-levels fall...)

With total welfare benefits rising in value at an average annual post-inflation rate of 8% from 1965 to 1972, pressures on wages fell correspondingly.

Meanwhile, though military spending rose absolutely, it fell to just 14% of the total 1978 budget. Highway construction fell to 3% of the Federal budget, while other new construction also slowed impressively.

Finally, productivity began to fall. The size of the pie — GNP per worker — slowed to just 0.9% annual growth from 1966 to 1980, after growing at an annual rate of 2.6% from 1947 to 1966.

All in all, it was less than a pretty picture. Plagued by inflationary locusts and uncertain of future profits, business felt alarmed. It is natural, then, that business leaders began to rethink the liberal strategy. No Reagan or Goldwater was needed as Cassandra. The situation spoke for itself.

Post-Liberal Capitalism?

It is clearly premature to say that the liberal era is over. Few current reversals of liberal policies are irreversible. Nevertheless, unless current trends change, liberalism *is* on the way out.

Initially, key architects of the new post-liberalism were leading multinational businessmen in search of a more stable profit environment. Welfare, labor costs, Third World pressures, and avoidable competition were targeted for reduction.

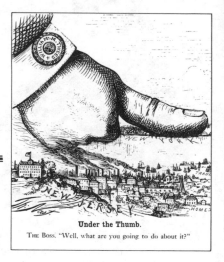

Under the Thumb.
THE BOSS. "Well, what are you going to do about it?"

Two primary committees formed with these aims in mind: the Trilateral Commission and the Committee on the Present Danger. One supported Carter, the other Reagan.

The Trilateral Commission formed first. Proposed in 1972 by David Rockefeller (then chair of Chase Manhattan Bank), the Trilateral Commission held its 180-member founding convention in 1973. It is " trilateral" in the sense that its members are key financiers and industrialists from the three main centers of the capitalist world: Western Europe, the U.S., and Japan.

The purpose of the Trilateral Commission is to formulate common solutions to joint trilateral problems of inflation, labor management, etc. President Carter once enthused that World War 2 might never have happened if the Trilateral Commission had existed before 1940...

The Trilateral Commission quickly attracted many prominent invited members. Besides Rockefeller, the North American section in 1973 included such men as Zbigniew Brzezinski (a close Rockefeller associate and later Commission Director); Cyrus Vance, a Wall Street lawyer and *NY Times* director; Senator Walter Mondale, originally a Hubert Humphrey protege; W. Michael Blumenthal, chair of the Bendix Corporation; Harold Brown, an IBM director and president of the California Institute of Technology; J. Paul Austin, chair of Coca-Cola; Bank of America president A.W. Clausen, now World Bank president; and various others.

HOW BOUT AN ICE COLD WAR?

Brown

Blumenthal

Most of these names should be familiar from the Carter Administration. Brzezinski became Carter's hard-line National Security Adviser. Vance became Secretary of State. Mondale became Vice-President. Blumenthal became Treasury Secretary. Brown became Defense Secretary. All told, 20 members of the Trilateral Commission became high Carter appointees.

Why did so many Trilateralists win high Carter positions? In brief, because the Trilateral Commission was vital to Carter's success. Without Trilateral aid, Carter probably would have remained an obscure regional politician. *With* Trilateral support, Carter emerged as a figure of national stature.

Accepted into the Trilateral fold in mid-1975, Carter gained financing, a favorable press, and (perhaps most importantly) a post-liberal rhetoric and strategy.

Zbigniew Brzezinski had written in 1973 that the 1976 Democratic candidate "will have to emphasize work, the family, religion, and increasingly, patriotism, if he has any desire to be elected."

Samuel Huntington, Brzezinski's close collaborator and later security planning coordinator for Carter's National Security Council, added a crucial proviso: "...The inside road to political office" belongs to "the 'outsider' in politics, or the candidate who could make himself or herself appear to be an outsider..."

Seeing a "high risk of global anarchy" in the post-Nixon years, with an inherent potential for "long-term disaster," Trilateralists feared that in some capitalist countries "the existing social and political system could be endangered."

With this in mind, the Commission hoped to promulgate policies and educate politicians to influence governments. This they achieved. Trilateralists have held high posts in many key Western countries...

In the U.S. David Rockefeller decided that the Commission needed a "New South" politician. Austin, whose Coca-Cola Company is based in Georgia, recommended Carter. Director Brzezinski agreed.

"Do you know me?"

Carter had been groomed by Coca-Cola for some time. Free travel on Coca-Cola executive jets brought Carter to meetings abroad and around the country in the early 1970's. Said Carter in 1974:

"We have our own built-in State Department in the Coca-Cola Company. They provide me ahead of time with...penetrating analyses of what the country is, what its problems are...and when I arrive there, provide me with an introduction to the leaders..."

The Trilateral Commission picked up where Coca-Cola left off. Brzezinski wrote many of Carter's campaign speeches, and Trilateral-owned media gave Carter's words special attention. *Time* magazine and the *New York Times* were particularly influential.

Prior to 1975, virtually no one outside Georgia knew of James Earl Carter. After joining the Commission in 1975, Carter rose from obscurity to become a popular sensation in early 1976.

What made Carter unique was not just that he was an "outsider" — the first president from the Deep South since Zachary Taylor in the 1850's — but that he jettisoned traditional Democratic politics.

All other Democratic nominees of the recent past have been classic liberals: McGovern (1972), Humphrey (1968), Johnson (1964), Kennedy (1960), Stevenson (1956, 1952). Carter, however, tried to meld a tough foreign policy with a "fiscally conservative" domestic policy. This made him not just a Republican in Democratic disguise — the typical judgement of many critics — *but an incipient post-liberal.*

Significantly more than Nixon, Carter tried to *shift the balance* from welfare to warfare.

Not one Carter appointee came from the 141-member Committee on the Present Danger — an oversight which Ronald Reagan rectified with a vengeance. Comparable to the Trilateral Commission in some respects, the Present Danger group takes a harder, more illiberal line both at home and abroad. Nevertheless, the overlap between Trilateralists and the Present Danger group is closer than might be imagined. Jointly, the two committees seek several objectives:

Internationally, all business leaders now want restored power and stability for multinational capital. Whether the U.S. is to be incontrovertibly supreme (the Present Danger goal) or "first among equals" (the Trilateral goal), the motive is essentially the same: ascendancy for U.S. business and its allies.

Nationally, all business leaders endorse the employers' offensive against labor now underway. Every kind of "takeback" that business can impose on labor is applauded. Says *Fortune:* employers want to "put a moratorium on social programs designed to redistribute income." They also want to put new limits on wages, unionism, etc.

The result is a post-liberal politics with very tangible consequences.

As a labor leader commented in 1978,

"I believe leaders of the business community, with few exceptions, have chosen to wage a one-sided class war in this country — a war against working people, the unemployed, the minorities, the very young and the very old, even many in the middle class of our society."

War spending has spiralled into the stratosphere under both Carter and Reagan. Labor unions have been trampled, as one contract after another has been revised to better serve the profit motive. Poverty rates, which began to increase under Carter (after a long slow decline), have skyrocketed under Reagan.

While median family earnings from 1972 to 1980 kept even with inflation only because so many families enrolled a second wage-earner in the labor market, average corporate profits in the same period rose 95% after inflation.

In 1970 the U.S. placed first in worldwide living standards (gross domestic product per capita). In 1980 the U.S. placed tenth.

True for the U.S. under Carter, this portrayal of the employers' offensive is doubly true for the U.S. under Reagan.

Carter's administration was in some ways a post-liberal experiment, with mixed results. Policies were started which still prevail, but Carter's personal approach to these policies was rebuffed.

In the economic sphere, Carter appointed Trilateralist Paul A. Volcker to preside over a recession as Fed chair. Volcker, formerly a Rockefeller employee at Chase Manhattan, did what he was asked. The idea was to stage Carter's recession at just the proper moment, so that a recovery would be underway by the 1980 election.

Washington Forum president Edwin Garlich, a Republican business leader, called this "a stroke of genius...perhaps even the makings of a two-term presidency. If Carter gets the economic slowdown early, then a pickup in late '79 and '80 and he brings inflation down, he'll look terrific in an election year."

Unfortunately for Carter, this recession was mistimed. Starting too late in Carter's term, it did not generate a recovery by November, 1980. Voters were not amused.

Reagan learned Carter's lesson well. Reagan started and finished a deeper, longer recession in time for the 1984 election.

Volcker served Reagan just as he had served Carter; Reagan showed his debt to Carterism by reappointing Volcker as Fed chair...

This brings us to...

REAGANOMIC$ (and the $upply $ide)

The pivot of Reagan's program was a "supply-side" miracle cure for stagflation — the ostensible "success" of which has helped Reagan stay popular. Is Reaganomics in fact successful?

A story from a Russian Jewish village of the Tsarist era offers an analogy...

A poor villager claps a hand to his forehead in despair. His wife and five children are crowded into a tiny hut. The din is maddening. Depressed, the villager asks his rabbi, "What can I do?" The rabbi answers: "Bring in your ducks, your geese, your goat." "But I shall go mad!" the man protests. "Do as I say," the rabbi orders.

Two weeks later the man returns in great distress. "My hut is so crowded I'm suffocating! Tell me, please, what can I do?" "Remove the ducks and the goat. Then wait a few days and come back."

The poor villager returns beaming. "No ducks! No goat! Rabbi, thank you — your advice worked wonders."

Reaganomics eliminates a few ducks.

After worsening the economy drastically, Reagan then describes a weak ensuing recovery as a new dawn. His *modus operandi* is clear: push the economy two steps back, then take credit for the single forward step which follows.

Take unemployment. Joblessness rose so high under Reagan (to 10.8% at one point) that when it returned to levels just slightly higher than when Reagan started, this return was greeted as a victory.

Similarly with interest rates.

Overall, the results of Reaganomics are clear: inflation temporarily slowed by an average unemployment rate unprecedented since the Great Depression; higher interest rates than ever before; profit gains without productivity gains; and deficits of astronomic proportions, the consequence of military spending hikes even larger than the savage cuts in social spending.

Is the economy profoundly healthier now than in 1980? No, despite Reagan's claims. The twin dragons of inflation and recession are still kicking...

Inflation, temporarily sluggish, will accelerate anew when the effects of Federal deficit spending are felt. So will interest rates. Even key Reagan aides concede this.

Joblessness, a scandal at 7.4% when Reagan entered office, is now celebrated at 8%. (One prime Reagan objective, in fact, seems to be redefining "full employment" as 7-8% unemployment.)

Has Reaganomics stimulated saving and investment? No. Consumer saving fell to a 33-year low in 1983, as inflation and tax "bracket creep" eliminated most public gains from Reagan's 1981 tax cut.

The wealthy and big business — the big gainers from the 1981 tax cut — chose *not* to invest in new production. Top-flight corporate mergers substituted for new products and jobs.

All this to the contrary notwithstanding, Reagan trumpets his modest "victory" over inflation...

Though the author of an orthodox trade-off between jobs and prices — spiced by a shift from welfare to warfare — Reagan poses as a magician capable of restraining *both* inflation and recession. The roots of this pose go back into Reagan's past...

Once upon a time Reagan was unabashedly pro-recession. As late as 1975 he pushed traditional Republicanism:

"We have to be able to accept that unemployment is going to rise before we can get over the disease of inflation...Recessions are only the pockmarks that come from the disease."

At this stage Reagan made light of joblessness: "It's a traumatic thing to be without a job and need and want one. But when you read that 50,000 of the laid-off Michigan auto workers had their unemployment checks sent to them in Florida all winter, you begin to wonder how much great distress there was."

To win the presidency, though, Reagan needed a line better suited to appeal to working voters. Supply-side doctrine filled the bill.

Promising gain without pain, supply-side rhetoric is just what the doctor ordered for gifted politicians in search of supporters. Said Reagan upon election:

"We don't have to choose between inflation and unemployment — they go hand in hand." Just trust "the magic of the marketplace," and both dragons of the economy will be slain...

So went Reagan's campaign line. The so-called theoretical basis for this line was sketched by USC economist Arthur Laffer on a napkin in November, 1974, for the benefit of *Wall Street Journal* writer Jude Wanniski.

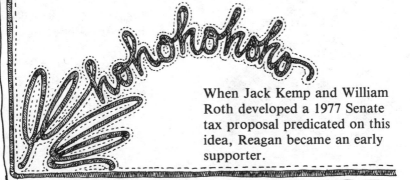

Wanniski then publicized the famous Laffer Curve, which purports to show that, at an ideal point, reduced business taxes lead to expanded investment by "the supply side" (business).

The beauty of the supply side scheme is that it promises rewards to business without (at first) seeming to jeopardize labor or the poor.

When Jack Kemp and William Roth developed a 1977 Senate tax proposal predicated on this idea, Reagan became an early supporter.

In office, Reagan quickly linked Kemp-Roth tax cuts to a double dose of defense hikes and social service cuts. This package, he promised in February, 1981, would yield "renewed optimism" and "robust growth" — specifically, "millions" of new jobs, sharply lowered prices, higher private saving, reduced taxes, and raised living standards.

Treasury Secretary Regan was even more specific, telling Congress that investment would rise 11% faster than inflation for at least five years.

The sun and the moon were nigh...

The Sorcerer's Apprentice

The wizard of Reagan's supply-side binge was budget director David Stockman. Stockman felt that the ills of the economy sprang essentially from production anarchy, i.e., firms acting individualistically, with no joint plan for revitalized production. His hope was that windfall tax breaks would prompt business to open its doors for coordinated new investment in line with Reagan administration plans...

Stockman's supply-side faith in business was clearly mystical. Senate majority leader Baker called the 1981 tax cut a "riverboat gamble." Reagan's pollster Richard Wirthlin agreed: "It *is* a gamble."

"Stockman is gambling on his ability to induce structural social change in the long run. His poker chips on the table are what happens in the short run."

"The whole thing is premised on faith."

"The markets will respond to that. Unless they are absolutely perverse."

In the short run, business was expected to respond to the tax cut with new investments. "That sets off adjustments and changes in perception that cascade through the economy. You have a bull market in '81, after April, of historic proportions."

This would be "a fiscal revolution:" priming supply (business) rather than demand (public and private buying, *a la* Keynes). Stockman was buoyantly confident:

Supply-side tax policies *did* work on one level — business enjoyed an unprecedented season of tax breaks. But Stockman's economic millenium did not come. Promised new investments never materialized.

Instead, business took its tax breaks and ran. Wall Street felt so sure that Reaganism did not portend a secure investment climate that the banks lifted the prime interest rate to 20.5% in August, 1981 — less than a month after Reagan proclaimed "the beginning of a new renaissance in America" with the passage of his so-called "Economic Recovery Tax Act."

A stock market slump, not a boom, was the immediate result of the Kemp-Roth tax cut. Predicting a recession, Treasury Secretary Donald Regan was frustrated:

"I must stand here today and ask, 'Where is the business response? Where are the expansion plans?' It's like dropping a coin down a well. All I'm hearing is an empty clink."

Far more than a coin went down the well, but the economy still did not revive. Two million people lost jobs in the six months after Reagan's tax cut. Interest rates went through the roof; real-estate sales collapsed; the housing industry fell to a new low; and auto sales disappeared. When the dust had settled, the economy had fallen lower than at any time since the Great Depression.

Stock Market 1, Stockman 0

When the supply-side bubble burst in autumn, 1981, David Stockman finally learned wisdom. Just months earlier Stockman had given the self-described "wild men" of the supply-side — Laffer, Gilder, Kemp — unqualified praise...

Gilder's supply-side bible, *Wealth and Poverty,* had been described by Stockman as "Promethean in its intellectual power." Reagan, too, pushed Gilder, displaying *Wealth and Poverty* on national television.

Now, Stockman retreated: "The supply-siders always had this magic view of the economy. That is, you could go from what was really a mess to nirvana in about a year and a half without any missteps...

Gilder, Laffer, and others stayed true to the faith, but most Reaganauts agreed that the experiment was over. Supply-side miracles were in short supply.

On October 18, 1981, Reagan officially conceded the arrival of "a slight recession and I hope a short recession." A slight and short hope!

Starting with a pro-recession bias, and saddled with a major recession, the Reaganauts decided to aim for an election-year recovery.

MAGIC ELIXIR! MIRACLE CURE! JUST A TASTE OF "REAGAN'S BITTER MEDICINE" DOES WONDERS FOR AN AILING ECONOMY. STEP RIGHT UP! COME ONE! COME ALL!

"Carter's Depression" — this was the phrase Reagan had used in 1980 to encapsulate the situation Carter created with his tight money policy. Reagan's depression now proved exceptionally deep. Managing this depression was not made easier by Reagan's stubborn refusal to abandon supply-side panaceas...

Among Reaganauts, Reagan was the last to give up on Gilder's gilded age. At issue were the vast deficits prompted by Reagan's tax giveaway to business. Without spending cuts commensurate to the 1981 tax cut, deficits were sure to soar — stimulating interest rates and depressing production.

Wall Street was the first to reject Lafferomics. Typical was the September, 1981, comment of a Dean Witter executive: "The new supply-side view is that deficits don't matter. *We* think that they do..."

Reagan resisted, hoping that deficits would fall even *with* giant war spending and smaller tax revenues. "Once...Reagan wondered aloud why the Fed did not simply reduce the prime rate...Apparently he had forgotten, or did not know, that the private banks rather than the Fed set the prime rate." Nearly two years passed before Stockman *et al.* could convince Reagan that deficits would not fall by themselves. In *Gambling With History,* journalist Laurence Barrett shows that virtually every Republican luminary tried to dissuade Reagan of supply-side fantasy — top aides, every key Senate supporter, Laxalt, Stockman, and most Cabinet members.

Reagan Good!   Carter Bad!   Blame Carter's   little liver pills!

During his 1980 campaign Reagan had chastised Carter for 7.4% unemployment: "I think the Federal Government has created this recession in its attempt to fight inflation by doing what the President swore up and down he would not do — by using unemployment as a tool."

Reagan, too, swore up and down that he would not use unemployment as a tool. His 1980 platform "specifically rejects the philosophy of the Carter administration that unemployment is the answer to inflation." By 1983, though, Paul Volcker expressly admitted that inflationary trends had briefly subsided only "under the heavy pressure of deep recession."

Above all, "Reaganomics" has consisted of *monetarism* — tight money policies forcing interest rates and joblessness *up* to keep demand and prices down — not (after the first fling) supply-side gambles. Volcker forced interest rates so exceptionally high that potential new production and employment were strangled in the cradle.

The precedent for this, as Robert Lekachman points out, was Margaret Thatcher as well as Jimmy Carter: "Until very recently, no democratic government, liberal or conservative, encouraged or ordered its central bank to pursue price stability at all costs. In the spring of 1979, Mrs. Thatcher did embark on such a journey. At the start of 1981, Ronald Reagan joined her."

The severity of Reagan's recession should have come as no surprise; Thatcher had already presided over 12.4% unemployment, England's worst rate since the 1930's.

What makes Reaganomics unique is not just monetarism and recession *per se,* but Reagan's special extras: tax cuts for business; service cuts for the needy; and unprecedented war spending.

The Tax Cut

Vice-President George Bush once denied that he had called Reagan's supply-side talk "voodoo economics." NBC TV refreshed his memory by showing a film clip of the remark — which remains just as accurate as it is unpalatable for Bush.

The victims of Reagan's voodoo are clear: all poor and working people who neither gain from the tax cut nor profit from social service cuts.

Who did gain from the 1981 tax cut?

Not the majority of the U.S. public. Thanks to several factors — low income-tax breaks for workers, upped gas and Social Security taxes, and "bracket creep" — 1981 taxpayers who earned less than $30,000 received zero or negative net tax gains.

Bracket creep is all too familiar. Say, for example, that your annual income rises exactly in step with inflation. Though your effective real income does not rise — you can buy no more than before — *your taxes do rise*. In this way, taxes rise as a proportion of income.

A family which earns $10,000 one year and $13,500 four years later — exactly keeping abreast of 35% inflation — pays a higher rate of real taxes in the latter year than in the former (5.5% compared to 3.7%). Hence a net loss results — you can buy *less* now than before.

Projections at the time of the 1981 tax cut made it clear that 48% of the public would have *higher* tax liabilities in 1984 than in 1981, while 31% would experience no real change. (Reagan's claim was that by 1984 taxes would be significantly lower for almost everyone.) Only the remaining 21% of the public, with 1981 incomes above $30,000, were expected to gain from Kemp-Roth. And even here average gains for people with 1981 incomes between $30,000 and $50,000 were projected to total just $84 per person.

Far and away the majority of Reagan's income-tax breaks — worth an estimated $9 billion — accrued to people with annual incomes above $50,000...

This was hardly an accident. As David Stockman conceded. "Kemp-Roth was always a Trojan horse to bring down the top rate."

"The hard part of the supply-side tax cut is dropping the top rate from 70% to 50%; the rest of it is secondary."

With Reagan's powerful support, Kemp-Roth became law. The top rate did indeed fall from 70% to 50%. The idea was that a fat bonus for the wealthy would "trickle down" to the public at large in the form of new investments, jobs, etc. Said Stockman:

"It's kind of hard to sell 'trickle down,' so the supply-side formula was the only way to get a tax policy that was really 'trickle down.'"

As a leading Democrat once said, trickle-down amounts to "feeding the horse so that pretty soon the sparrows will get something to eat, too."

Whatever may have descended from Reagan's Trojan horse to the public, at least one thing is certain: corporations and the wealthy came out smelling like roses. An estimated $750 billion in Federal tax cuts over five years has streamed almost entirely into business coffers.

It may be doubted whether Reagan's investment and tax credits were strictly calculated to optimize production. Though the top 1700 U.S. firms have created just 4% of the new jobs in the last 20 years, precisely these firms received 80% of Reagan's corporate tax breaks. These firms then neglected new production for a merger spree which accounted for 1807 transactions worth $61 billion in the first three quarters of 1981 alone.

Since 1981, mergers have continued with spectacular regularity, most visibly in the oil and steel industries. The rich get richer...and the big get bigger.

Said David Stockman: "Do you realize the greed that came to the forefront? The hogs were really feeding. The greed level, the level of opportunism, just got out of control."

Let's eat!

And don't forget to enrich yourselves!

The War on the Poor

Giving to the rich requires taking from the poor.

Committed to $750 billion *less* in Federal intake (thanks to the 1981 tax cut) and to an over 50% hike in war spending from 1981 to 1985, the Reagan administration enjoys only one form of spending restraint: slashed services for the needy.

Zealous about serving the wealthy — above all, by expanding ultra-profitable war production — Reagan is equally zealous about zapping the poor.

"Rarely has compassion been so mistaken for its opposite."

This was Edwin Meese's complaint in December, 1983, when Reagan and Meese came under fire for doubting the existence of U.S. hunger. Meese protested that Reagan is no Scrooge — and that even Scrooge, the flint-hearted villain of *A Christmas Carol,* gets "a bad press"...

"If you really look at the facts, Scrooge didn't exploit Bob Cratchit. So let's be fair to Scrooge. He had his faults, but he wasn't unfair to anyone."

How about Reagan?

Volumes could be written about Reagan's frenetic assault on the poor. The main points are these: Overall, Reagan has cut social programs by $110 billion since 1981. The Congressional Budget Office reports that 40% of all losses were suffered by families with less than $10,000 in yearly income. 70% of total losses accrued to households with incomes under $20,000.

How much is $110 billion? Listen to David Stockman:
"Do you have any idea what $40 billion means? It means I've got to cut the highway program, milk-price supports, and Social Security student benefits. And education and student loans. And manpower training and housing and the synfuels program.

"I put together a list of 20 social programs that had to be zeroed out completely, like Job Corps, Head Start, women and children's feeding programs, on and on. And another 25 that have to be cut by 50%...I mean really fierce, blood-and-guts stuff — widows benefits and orphans benefits, things like that. And still it didn't add up to $40 billion."

$110 billion is *really* fierce.

Exceptionally important to the poor, programs to promote health, education, welfare, and employment are also relatively cheap. Furnishing nearly 50% of the 1981 income of the bottom 20% of the population, social services use just 10% of Federal resources.

Few other programs benefit so many for so little. Yet precisely these programs have borne the brunt of Reaganite cuts. In 1982, low-income people lost 2½ times more services than other households. So too in 1983 and 1984, in myriad service fields.

Poverty levels which began rising in 1978 continued to rise steeply under the impact of Reaganomics. The Census Bureau reported in late 1983 that 34.4 million people — 15% of the population — fell a total of $43 billion below the official 1982 poverty line for a family of four ($9862). Not since 1965 had the situation been worse.

Just four years earlier, the poverty rate had been 11.4%. The increase to 15% meant that *10 million* people had newly fallen into official poverty.

Reagan's policy bears special responsibility for increased poverty since Reaganism unequally affects not only the poor, but people just above the poverty line. In 1982, 20-25 million people just over the poverty line lost either income, in-kind benefits, or public jobs. When CETA job training was cancelled, 400,000 people left the "working poor" to join the poor in one fell swoop.

Reagan's anti-welfare passion is well known. In friendly company, Reagan even cracks jokes about it.

When David Stockman was scheduled to present Congress with the proposed 1981 service cuts, Reagan kidded: "We won't leave you out there alone, Dave. We'll all come to the hanging."

Presidential counsellor James Baker also poked fun at Stockman's image: "We saved a lot of air-conditioning in the White House this summer. We kept cool by huddling around Dave Stockman's heart."

One budget proposal was nicknamed the "rape, pillage, and burn option."

As California governor, Reagan declared what Ed Meese called "all-out war on the taxtaker." Sharp reductions in innumerable programs — mental health, food aid, etc. — were complemented by classic Reagan lines: Welfare recipients, he said, are "a faceless mass waiting for handouts." "Unemployment insurance is a pre-paid vacation for freeloaders."

Reagan now accuses his critics of "greed and envy." Criticized for lack of compassion, Reagan is quick to strike back: "I've heard all that crap. We haven't thrown anyone out in the snow to die." In May, 1983, Reagan unburdened himself: "I get a little irritated with that constant refrain about compassion. I got an unsigned valentine in February and I'm sure it was from Fritz Mondale. The heart on it was bleeding."

Reagan's heart clearly does not bleed for poor or working people. Take his famous pledge to protect "the truly needy." Seven programs ("the safety net") were defined as immune from Stockman's flashing knife: Medicare, veterans pensions, Social Security old-age benefits, school meals, home relief, Head Start, and summer youth jobs.

Almost without exception these programs were later cut. $18 billion, e.g., vanished from the Federal health budget — taken mainly from Medicare.

Many of Reagan's sharpest cuts have been directed against AFDC (Aid to Families with Dependent Children). This is not surprising, given Reagan's campaign rhetoric about "welfare queens in designer jeans;" still, it makes scant economic or moral sense.

Very little of the Federal budget goes to AFDC. In 1979, with states and localities bearing part of the cost, 11 million AFDC recipients received an average of $93 per person per month. That equaled about $4500 per year for a family of four, accounting (in aggregate) for just over 1% of the Federal budget. 63% of AFDC recipients were children, almost all with single mothers; the majority had received aid for less than three years.

Of the six million people aged 21-63 who received disability pay in 1980, more than one million were targeted by Reagan for outright termination...Is it a surprise that the deaf sign for "Reagan" is a revolver pointed at the head?

Food and nutrition programs have been another key Reagan target — again with meager justification...

FOOD 1 STAMP

Food stamps have been remarkably cost-effective — i.e., underfunded.

Average daily benefits in 1981 equaled just 44ᶜ a meal, which (though tiny) meant a great deal to recipients averaging just $3900 in 1981 income.

Reagan was merciless with food stamps. Year one of his budget cuts saw a $2.3 billion food stamp reduction, with roughly a million people terminated. Later years saw even sterner measures. In 1983, for example, Reagan asked for the termination of 3 million recipients, with funding cuts for another 14 million. Cost-of-living increases were postponed and levels of income eligibility fell.

Meals for schoolchildren have also been slashed. Intended to give poor children meals meeting at least one-third of their nutritional needs, the Federal lunch program was cut on the basis of an absurdly flimsy pretext — that catsup counts as a vegetable for health purposes! When asked about this, Reagan's Agricultural Secretary responded:

"I think it would be a mistake to say that catsup *per se* was classified as a vegetable. Catsup in combination with other things was classified as a vegetable." What other things? "French fries or hamburgers."

Small wonder that Reagan declared himself "perplexed" when presented with evidence of U.S. hunger.

Earlier, Reagan joined Ed Meese in claiming that people go to soup kitchens not because they're hungry — there is no "authoritative" evidence of hunger, said Meese — but simply to take advantage of the free food.

Still earlier, Reagan won renown for a remark about a free food giveaway forced by a terrorist group:

"It's just too bad we can't have an epidemic of botulism!"

At least one major Reagan budget cut misfired badly — a bold effort to slash Social Security.

Supposedly to prevent the "most devastating bankruptcy in history...on or about November 3, 1982," Reagan and Co. proposed $82 billion in Social Security cuts, including the elimination of minimum benefits for 3 million people; when this proved unpopular, they proposed $40 billion in cuts. This too proved unacceptable to the public.

Undaunted, Reagan then pretended that he had never challenged Social Security: "I will not stand by and see those of you are dependent on Social Security deprived of your benefits."

"My Hypocritic Oath?? Sure — close my heart and hope they die!!!"

1982's "devastating bankruptcy" was completely averted by an interfund transfer; it turned out that just one *branch* of Social Security had been cash-poor...

Reagan's 1985 budget projects $9 billion in cuts: $2.7 billion from Medicare and Civil Service retirement programs; $3 billion from AFDC and the food stamp program; and $3 billion from other domestic programs. Even more radical is another administration plan, floated on March 15, 1984 — calling for *$43* billion in new domestic cuts.

Balance Sheet

Reagan's economic rhetoric has been consistently euphoric. Reaganomic realities have been another matter.

In September, 1983, Reagan railed at his critics: "We've got a recovery train going, and rather than whine and carp and complain, the misery merchants should get on board." Is Reagan's recovery train on track? Judge for yourself:

In 1980, Reagan promised a balanced budget by 1984 and budget surpluses afterwards. Instead, he authorized profligate war spending leading to unprecedented budget deficits.

- Reagan's projected 5-year deficit from 1981 through 1985 is *$727.6 billion* — higher than the sum total of all U.S. deficits since George Washington.

- The Federal debt rose so fast — 51% from 1981 to 1984 — that Reagan was forced to raise the Federal debt ceiling to a record $1.49 trillion. Interest on the national debt (paid to banks) now commands 12.7% of total Federal outlays.

- The *increase* in this interest since 1981 exceeds the total saved by *all* Reaganite cuts in health, education, welfare, and social services — by $14 billion through 1985.

In November, 1982, Reagan changed his tune on budget-balancing: "I've never said anything but that it was a goal."

Once a promise, now a goal; in any event, the balanced budget is more distant now than ever...

According to the AP on February 16, 1984: "President Reagan said yesterday that he does not think the projected $180 billion budget deficit next year poses a serious threat to the economic recovery, or is responsible for high interest rates or the decline on Wall Street." Very few people agree. Volcker and almost all Wall Street analysts say precisely the opposite.

In 1980, Reagan himself repeatedly claimed that inflation arises from "government spending more than government takes in." In 1975, he was caustic on the same subject: "When George Meany testifies to Congress that this country can afford a $100 billion deficit to solve the unemployment problem, it's obvious that he's been the victim of bad advice. If we overspend by $100 billion now, he'll be back asking that we overspend by $250 billion the next time. When government uses a deficit to create work, it also creates inflation."

For Reagan, apparently, it seems that using a deficit to create weapons is *not* inflationary. His proposed 1985 war budget is $313 billion. The beat goes on...

Stockman, characteristically blunt, says that the U.S. may soon be in the "position of many companies on the eve of Chapter 11" (i.e., verging on bankruptcy). Chrystler Corporation president Lee Iacocca complains about the deficit: "It's screwy, it's out of control...It's going to destroy our competitiveness." Business is finally beginning to worry. Though Reaganomic revelry has been a profiteers' delight, it now seems likely to entail unpleasant consequences.

Unpleasant consequences are nothing new for Reagan's primary scapegoats: racial minorities, women, the poor, labor. Affected harshly and unequally by Reaganomic austerity, these groups have attracted special Reagan attention. The pleasure is all his...

Discriminating Tastes

The Black Community has been especially hard-hit by the recessions of 1974-75, 1979-80, and 1981-82. From 1972-1983, Black unemployment rose from an already steep 10.3% to 20.2%. Black family income fell 8.3%. Of the 26.5 million Black citizens counted by the 1980 Census, 8.9 million were officially poor (34%).

With Reagan in office, the plight of Blacks has grown measureably worse. This is less than surprising, given his record...

"We'll settle for the white vote." Thus spoke an aide in Reagan's 1966 gubernatorial campaign. For a campaign largely premised on racial polarization, this was far from an aberrant comment. Said strategist Stuart Spencer: "We knew Ron wasn't going to get anywhere with Negroes..."

In 1966, the U.S. was enmeshed in an upsurge of racial tension. A Black exodus from the south in the 1950's had brought nearly 1.5 million Black workers into new labor markets. Roughly a quarter of these emigrants had come to California. With a tenfold increase in the Black population of Los Angeles and similar increases elsewhere, a dual movement arose: *against* racial discrimination—and for it.

"Civil rights" militancy met "white backlash" in a head-on collision. Acute tensions resulted both from insurgent political organizing and from spontaneous inner-city riots (in Watts, Detroit, etc.).

Reagan's political identity crystallized at a time when right politics and white backlash were practically synonymous. Like Goldwater, Reagan opposed the Federal Civil Rights acts of 1964 and 1965. When he ran for governor, the most hotly contested California issue was "fair housing," *i.e.,* stopping racial discrimination in housing. Ronald Reagan opposed fair housing.

When Reagan spoke to the California Real Estate Association, he charged that Blacks who alleged discrimination "staged attempts to rent homes, when in truth there was no real intention of renting, only of causing trouble."

Rising to philosophic heights, Reagan posited that the "right of an individual to the ownership and disposition of property is inseparable from the right of freedom itself."

As governor, Reagan told a group of Black legislators:

"You wouldn't want
to sell your house to a
red-headed Kiwanian if
you didn't want to,
would you?"

In short, for Reagan, freedom to discriminate is more vital than freedom *from* discrimination; property rights take precedence over civil rights.

Though Reagan once denied the very existence of white backlash, he navigated its shoals and rapids with great success. In a candid moment, strategist Bill Roberts contended that Reagan's campaign was superior to that of his Democratic opponent:

"The Democrats showed they were out of touch by going so hard on right-wing extremism. In 1966 the Birchers weren't throwing Molotov cocktails and hitting policemen; the Negroes were...The average Bircher looks, acts and talks pretty much like everybody else. If you meet him, say, at a cocktail party you're not going to start looking for a bomb shelter. When California was worried about Negro rioters, Pat Brown was talking about Birchers."

Ronald Reagan did not talk about Birchers.

"These are no longer riots connected with civil rights in any way. These are riots of the law breakers and the mad dogs against the people." So Reagan pontificated after the 1967 Detroit riots. Typically, he showed little interest in the poverty and oppression which spark riots.

Reagan's imagery began to grow lurid. He once compared Black militants who jeered Hubert Humphrey to the "jackbooted young monsters" of the Hitler Youth Corps. On several occasions he used "jungle" metaphors: "Every day the jungle draws a little closer," ran a radio ad. "Our city streets are jungle paths after dark..."

"Man's determination to live under the protection of the law has pushed back the jungle down through the centuries. But the jungle is always there, and somehow it seems much closer than we have known it in the years preceding."

The answer? Law and order: "With all our science and sophistication...the jungle still is waiting to take over. The man with the badge holds it back."

In 1968, pursuing the presidency, Reagan was asked: "Which views of George Wallace do you disagree with?" (In 1968 Wallace's name was synonymous with white bigotry.) Said Reagan:

> "Well, now, lately on the basis of his speeches that would be kind of hard to pin down because he's been speaking a lot of things that I think people of America are in agreement with. But I would have to say [that] he showed no opposition particularly to great programs of Federal aid and spending programs and so forth."

Stern words! **Ronald Reagan, civil rightist...**

Earlier, when civil rights hero Martin Luther King was assassinated during a 1968 Memphis labor dispute, Reagan linked King's death to civil disobedience: this "great tragedy," Reagan said, "began when we began compromising with law and order and people started choosing which laws they'd break." In other words, King was partly at fault for his own murder!

On the day of King's funeral, Reagan was less than eloquent; he said he hoped the new baseball season would "turn our minds to the better side of our national life. Baseball...in recent years has offered Negroes of athletic ability unparalleled chances for fame and success. I am pleased that it is now time to play ball." **Strike three?**

Civil Rights

Reagan often lets the cat out of the bag on racial matters — telling tasteless jokes about African cannibals, Chinese laundries, etc.; praising South Africa; calling anti-slavery martyr John Brown "a madman"; giving a televised 1976 address from the town where three civil rights workers were murdered; and so on. Nancy Reagan is equally unsubtle. In 1980, by amplified phone hookup from Chicago to New Hampshire, she wished aloud that Reagan could "see all these beautiful white people."

An occasional *faux pas* is one thing. More serious is presidential policy. Here, too, Reagan has been bad news for racial minorities.

A bird's-eye view of Reaganite civil rights policy is available through a glance at Reagan's conflict with the U.S. Commission on Civil Rights. On October 11, 1983, the Commission reported that the enforcement of civil rights laws had declined precipitously since 1981. Specifically, the Commission called attention to a 21% slide in the civil rights enforcement staff of six agencies: five Departments (Justice, Education, Labor, Health and Human Services, Housing and Urban Development) and the Equal Employment Opportunities Commission.

Two weeks later, Reagan fired three Civil Rights commissioners. Never before in the 26-year history of the commission had something similar occurred. Only a last-minute compromise kept the Commission alive at all.

Reagan now moved to pack the Commission,

- New chair Clarence Pendleton, a conservative San Diego businessman, was asked in January 1984 which groups are most victimized by discrimination. Pendleton suggested...Eastern Europeans!

- New staff director Linda Chavez persuaded the Commission to study "reverse discrimination" against the white European males instead of the effects of Reaganite cuts. She also initiated a study of the "radical" idea that men and women who perform equal work should receive equal pay, and told the press that discrimination is not one of the major problems facing Black people.

In the words of a White House aide, "Now that we have the Civil Rights Commission on our side, we can make use of them to run some interference for us."

Strong but unavailing objections came from the Leadership Conference on Civil Rights — a coalition of 160 women's, Hispanic, Black, and other groups. Conference leaders denounced the Chavez plan as something that "reads like the civil rights agenda of the Radical Right." No wonder. Reagan's civil rights track record is abysmal.

In 1982, the Justice Department announced major tax exemptions for 100 racially segregated schools and groups.

When this move proved unpopular, White House aides denied that Reagan had been responsible for it. Later, when a Reagan letter favoring the exemptions came to light Reagan said:

"No one put anything over on me...I'm the originator of the whole thing."

Non-enforcement of civil rights laws is a Reagan specialty. Typical is the view expressed in a letter by Terrell Bell, Education Secretary: "The courts may soon be after us for not enforcing civil rights laws and regulations. It seems that we have some laws we shouldn't have, and my obligation to enforce them is against my own philosophy."

Reagan opposed strengthening the Voting Rights Act; slashed affirmative action and bilingual education; attacked voluntary as well as mandatory school busing; and (by January, 1984) had initiated just one school desegregation suit.

So extreme is Reagan's approach to civil rights that even key Republican allies do not uniformly assent to it. Senator Bob Packwood, then chair of the Senate Republican Campaign Committee, expressed a telling fear: "The Republican Party has just about written off women who work for wages in the marketplace. We are losing them in droves. You cannot write them off and the Blacks and the Hispanics and the Jews and assume that you're going to build a party of white Anglo-Saxon males over forty. There aren't enough of us left."

Soon, there was one less. Packwood was dismissed from his Republican leadership post.

New Right/No Rights: Women

Reagan is very bad news for women and children, sharply reducing welfare payments to women. 69% of all foodstamp cuts, for example, affect members of households headed by single women. Similarly with cuts in public housing, legal services, etc. Virtually *all* AFDC cuts have the same effect. And Reagan has deleted funding for innumerable other programs important to women: child care, battered women's centers, and so on.

Since Reagan's election, 2.5 million women have fallen below the poverty line.

Reagan has never had a totally enlightened view of women. As California governor, he once received a remarkable diatribe qua letter: "Women need to be liberated like a humming bird needs a flight manual. What I'm saying is not against women...I love women...But I sneer at their current drive for liberation — whatever the hell that means...God made the first woman, Eve, from one of Adam's ribs...and I think that was where all the trouble started. It all boils down to simple jealousy!"

Responded Reagan: "I am pleased to tell you that I share your views about women's liberation...and above all, I want to thank you from the bottom of my heart for your letter."

Reagan's one brief lapse as an anti-feminist — brief 1972 support for the Equal Rights Amendment — was righted so completely that, when Reagan entered office in 1981, Phyllis Schafly rejoiced that this "kills the ERA."

With Reagan's help, the ERA fell. Reagan has also been an ardent anti abortionist.

Reagan is characteristically lax about sex discrimination. The Justice official assigned to review Federal laws for evidence of gender-based discrimination (Barbara Honegger) said in late 1983 that Reagan's promise to revise discriminatory laws is a "sham." "He has reneged on his commitment. Not a single law has been changed."

Reaganaut vengeance was swift: Honegger was disparaged as a "low-level munchkin" (Thomas DeCair), "the Easter Bunny at the White House Easter egg roll" (press secretary Larry Speakes). Speakes added:

"It's quite an admirable thing to do. It's not easy to dress up in that hot bunny suit. I've never done it and I'm ashamed to admit it."

Perhaps most telling of all is the Reaganaut decision in early 1984 to challenge a Federal court order instructing the State of Washington to compensate women for wages below the "full evaluated worth" of their work (using Washington criteria of "worth").

Sexual pay disparities are one of the most striking facts on the economic scene. For every dollar a working man earns, a working woman makes 59ᶜ. Women engineers make 68% of what male engineers earn ($371 per week vs. $547). Among sales workers, women earn just 52% as much as men ($190 per week vs. $366). And so it goes.

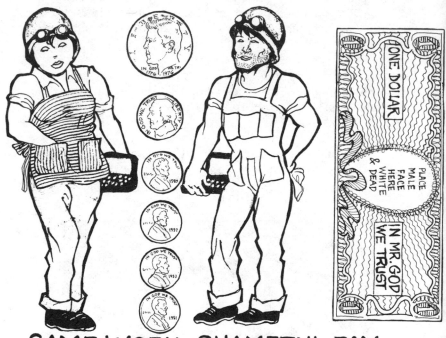

SAME WORK- SHAMEFUL PAY

Reagan and Co. show not the slightest desire to rock this boat. Eleanor Smeal, former president of the National Organization of Women, sees a direct connection between business gains from low pay and Reagan's hostility to the ERA, equal pay, etc. Not one trade association or chamber of commerce supported the ERA. Reagan is nothing if not pro-business.

Profits Before People

The ferocity of Reagan's campaign against welfare, minorities, and women becomes more comprehensible when we view it through the prism of his general pro-business bias. Keep a few basic points in mind:

1. Business pursues expanding profits.
2. Profits tend to expand when wages contract.
3. Wages tend to contract when welfare falls.

Until the 1970's, the size of the post-war economic pie rose so fast that U.S. business could pay rising wages to unionized labor without jeopardizing rising profits. As long as the pie grew faster than labor's share, the profit picture stayed bright.

U.S. business was *willing* to share with labor to ensure the political stability of the Rooseveltian coalition, which had vaulted the U.S. into world preeminence. Permitting unions a degree of prosperity gave them a stake in the exploitation of nonunion and foreign workers. The AFL-CIO thus became a pillar of the war establishment, always ready to endorse "police actions" abroad.

Few objections to war production came from relatively privileged war industry labor...

The 1970's economic crunch changed this capital/labor equation.

"A historical shift appears to be looming in the balance of power between labor and management. It is a shift that favors management by making strikes less likely, more costly, and in general less effective..."
Fortune magazine

Reagan's vendetta against welfare makes special sense in the light of the employers' offensive against labor. "There is," as Frank Ackerman says, "a method to this meanness: deprived of government benefits, workers will be forced to beg for jobs, to work for less than before." In 1975, Reagan urged precisely this:

"Maybe we need to get back the Depression mentality, where there were no menial jobs. A job was a job, and anyone who got one felt lucky."

As president, Reagan recreated this Depression mentality — by plunging the economy into what he once called "great depths of...depression" (a phrase he later tried to retract).

Both social services and living standards have fallen. At the peak of the recession in December, 1982, 20% of the labor force was either unemployed (12.6%, including 1.6 million "discouraged" workers omitted from unemployment statistics for failing to seek work), or underemployed (7.3%). In 1982, 25% of the workforce went officially without work for some part of the year.

Reagan administration support for anti-labor efforts has been unwearying. Thanks to recent enactments:

- The Professional Air Traffic Controllers Organization (PATCO) has been decertified for striking...an ominous lesson for all public workers unions (PATCO was one of the few unions to *support* Reagan in 1980.)

- Firms may now cancel labor agreements simply by moving from union to nonunion plants; this is only forbidden if existing agreements explicitly preclude such moves.

- Firms may now declare bankruptcy to void labor contracts — and then reorganize on a nonunion basis. (Continental Airlines did just this, laying off half its workforce and then cutting wages 50%!)

- Reagan aides proposed a Labor Department rule change that would allow state employment agencies to supply scab replacements to firms with striking or locked-out workers.

Merrily-Lynch 'Em
(Labor Consultants)

Bullish on Profits

Is it any wonder that, long ago, Reagan found himself denounced "at the top level of the AFL-CIO...as a 'strident voice of the right-wing lunatic fringe'"? Labor clearly has no reason to like Ronald Reagan.

"Fully half the union contracts signed since 1982 have given back to employers gains the unions had previously won..." (*Newsday*) *In toto,* all union workers in 1983 negotiated contracts 1.2% below the 1982 level — the steepest decline since recordkeeping started in 1967.

These figures would be unremarkable in much of the world, but for U.S. unions — the royalty of global labor — they represent a stunning blow. Contrary to popular mythology, 1980's "Big Labor" is neither fat, happy, nor aggressive...

In 1983, just 4,320 union elections were held — 59% of the 1980 tally. Only 43.8% of these elections were won by labor, a record low. Union membership, already below 20% of the workforce, is still falling. Considering the number of AFL-CIO givebacks, this decline is no great mystery. As Anthony Mazzocchi of the Oil, Chemical, and Atomic Workers union says, "Workers can see you don't need a union card to hold up a white flag."

In a nutshell, workers are on the defensive. The pace and tempo of the business offensive, fast under Carter, has quickened under Reagan.

Labor weakness springs from two sources: the great disunity of the working class; and the growing unity of the business class. No crystal ball is needed to predict the outcome of a situation in which friends fall out and foes link hands...

Proletarians, Unite?

In many respects, the global working class is more vital and irrepressible now than ever. To begin with, today's working class *is* global. In 1848, when Marx and Engels exhorted "the proletarians of all lands" to unite, very few lands outside Europe were populated by proletarians (wage-workers). As recently as 1940, after more than a century of capitalism (mass production for private profit), wage-workers were still concentrated largely in Europe and North America (with outposts but few heartlands elsewhere).

All this has now changed. Multinational business increasingly has a multinational labor pool at its disposal.

As a result, employers feel increasingly free to assail Big Labor. They know that 'Little Labor' will do comparable work for less pay. Steelworkers in

Brazil and computer assembly lines in Hong Kong make Youngstown and Silicon Valley expendable...

Until recently, Big Labor gloried in its relative privilege. Strong enough to wring concessions from Big Business — thanks to its 1930's organizing drives —

the AFL-CIO long ago realized that union fortunes depend on business success. Profits can only be *shared* when they *accumulate...*

And when profits are shared too widely, the benefits they confer become vanishingly small. Big Labor thus tried to keep the big *majority* of world labor outside its ranks. It succeeded perhaps too well.

For years, organized labor had prospered from Big Business exploitation of disorganized labor. But now, Little Labor displaces Big Labor. Multinational business is on the warpath against high-wage labor, secure in the knowledge that an ever more diversified pool of low-wage labor can be called upon. Big Labor is outnumbered.

To fight back, workers need vastly expanded global unity.

Big Labor and Little Labor need to accept and assist each other.

This will be anything but easy.

The union movement has been so narrow for so long that the very word "labor" now conjures up a narrow image. "Workers" are pictured in stereotyped terms as card-carrying blue-collar unionists.

Few images could be less valid. The working class extends far beyond unionized North American factories. Increasingly, wage-work for Big Business is performed by Asians, Africans, and Latin Americans; by women and children; in "high tech," low tech, high pay and low pay industries. Qualitatively more than ever, workers in all lands are now subjected to the same employers. Unity *now* would mean cross-national and cross-industry solidarity in opposition to giant employers.

Solidarnosc in Poland was a major step in this direction. If the Soviet Union had been unable to intervene, *Solidarnosc* would almost certainly have won state power. Collaboration between Polish and Russian workers could still make this possible. Similarly, collaboration between U.S., Japanese, Western European, and Third World workers would have immense potential.

The union Old Guard daydreams about past glories, but business is on another wavelength. To confront multinational capital, a multinational labor movement is called for. Such a movement will not be created easily — but what alternative do workers have?

The Demopublican Party

In the U.S., the public has grown accustomed to a very narrow spectrum of political debate. With Democrats in office, Republicans pose as an alternative. With Republicans in office, Democrats wait in the wings.

The difficulty with this vaudeville two-step is that neither party stands for a real alternative to war, exploitation, or poverty. Both Democrats and Republicans are committed to Big Business — a commitment which is increasingly dangerous in an era when Big Business pursues a global offensive not only against labor, but against the U.S.S.R., Libya, Nicaragua, etc.

We have seen that both Democrats and Republicans walked the warfare/welfare line. Similarly, both a Democrat (Carter) and a Republican (Reagan) initiated post-liberal policies — knitting wildly militarized anti-communism together with anti-welfare, anti-labor domestic policies.

Internationally, Democrats have been slightly more warlike than Republicans. JFK, the reigning Democratic saint, sent troops to Vietnam; sponsored the Bay of Pigs invasion of Cuba; accelerated the nuclear arms race; dared Krushchev to risk war during the Cuban missile crisis; fired propaganda salvos over the Berlin wall; etc.

Domestically, the Democratic-Republican tango is the longest running show off Broadway.

Democrats spark recession, winning the Republicans popularity; Republicans then spark recession, swinging the pendulum back to the Democrats. Carter and Reagan introduced a new step — a tap dance from mild to extreme recession...

This Demopublican jazzercise is ingenious, but it makes a basic underlying problem: the persistence and decreasing manageability of inflation, recession, the nuclear arms race, etc. If stagflation and war trends grow too serious, neither party will be able to save the situation.

Both parties now pursue a myopic strategy boosting short-term profits without solving problems of warfare or human welfare. Post-liberalism is still close to liberalism. Big business is served — while the economy and the nuclear arms race careen out of control...

The Democrats have pursued a dual path with Reagan in office: supporting the post-liberal business offensive while trying to assign all blame to Reagan.

BY THE TIME HE'S THROUGH, THE PUBLIC WILL WELCOME US BACK!

"He's running the government. We're not running the government." Thus spoke House Speaker Tip O'Neill when budget deficits began to run riot. The truth is quite different. Reagan's 1981 tax package, for example, attracted wide Democratic support. The Senate voted 89-11 in support of Reagan, while 48 Democrats gave Reagan a 43-vote margin of victory in the House.

As David Stockman observed, the original 70/50 proposal for reduced upper bracket taxes came from the Democrats. So had many other aspects of the tax cut. Just three days before the final vote, the *NY Times* reported this Demopublican scene:

"For every tax break the White House offered the rich and powerful, the Democrats offered one of their own, sometimes two...For the oil industry, the thrift banks...and those looking to duck estate taxes, there is no anxiety about the final vote on these bills. Heads or tails, they win."

The final bill, said Treasury Secretary Regan, "includes 95% of what the president wanted."

Did the Democrats whistle a different tune years later? Not in November, 1983, when 67 House Democrats voted *not* to restore $1 billion in slashed education and social service funding. (The final vote was 206 to 203.)

Finally, in 1984, the House majority leader James Wright (D-Texas) announced a Democratic plan to "recommend cuts in entitlement programs." Watch out, Medicare!

Democrats talk more readily about slower war spending than Reagan does, but few leading Democrats stray far from militarism:

Walter Mondale supports the Stealth bomber, the Midgetman missile, and a 4% annual war spending increase (just 1% less than Carter proposed in 1980; Carter now supports Mondale); Gary Hart opposed the Nuclear Freeze and wants what the media calls a "meaner, leaner" military; Senate "doves" Alan Cranston and Christopher Dodd, respectively, support the B1 nuclear bomber and the Neutron bomb; and Edward Kennedy responded to Reagan's 1984 request for an "emergency" $62 million for El Salvador — after protesting "giving a blank check to death squads and despotism — by urging a $21 million check!

After more than 6000 U.S./Russian arms meetings since World War II, the arms race continues faster than ever. As Daniel Ellsberg has shown, most central questions of arms limitation (e.g., sea-based missiles) have been ignored for at least a decade. Carter's SALT II approach was no more serious than Reagan's stalled START proposal (also endorsed by Carter).

The
Lesser
Evil

Not one leading Demopublican with a prayer of gaining party power offers the slightest real hope of disarmament. Verbal "freeze" pledges conceal a situation in which *very* few Demopublicans reject *present* levels of firepower. Like Republicans, Democrats accept both military anarchy and the business offensive.

For an alternative, working and poor people must rely on themselves. Neither post-liberalism nor liberalism offers a viable response to environmental crisis, the arms race, or economic insecurity.

2000%
overkill

5000%
overkill

Of the Rich, For the Rich, By the Rich

"Material wealth is God's way of blessing people who put Him first." Reverend Jerry Falwell

This Moral Majority gospel is music to Demopublican ears, especially to Ronald Reagan. So is the Golden Rule — i.e., "The Man with the Gold makes the Rules." Says a former aide: "Reagan's support is populist, but he's not. All his instincts are pro-big business."

In 1978, Reagan and Paul Laxalt were irked that Big Business PACs (political action committees) had given Democrats and Republicans roughly equal funding. Reagan complained (unfairly): "Why does half the business PAC money go to candidates who may not be friends of business?" Echoed Laxalt: "We found that our 'friends,' the *Fortune* 500, were playing both sides. When you push water for them as long as we have, that's a little hard to swallow." In 1980, Reagan saw little reason to complain: his buckets (and pockets) overflowed...

"We will mine more, drill more, cut more timber." This was James Watt's prophetic promise at the start of his years as Interior Secretary...

Watt has an unquenchable zest for making enemies. A high-octane rightist, Watt once distinguished two kinds of people — "liberals and Americans." Calling environmentalists "a left-wing cult," Watt assailed his opponents with all the fervor of a genuine religious fanatic. Soon, Watt personally became a major issue, ultimately forced from office for a careless remark. But behind Watt stood Reagan. As Reagan once told photographer Ansel Adams, "Jim's a pretty good Joe." When Watt came under fire, Reagan defended him zealously. After resigning, Watt called Reagan's new Interior Secretary (William Clark) "a fantastically fine guy."

After his election, Reagan recruited a fabulously wealthy team. Ten of his 1981 Cabinet members held assets which (combined) were valued at $38 million. Bush, Baker, and Clark are millionaire ranchers. Shultz and Regan earned *salaries* at Bechtel and Merrill-Lynch just under $1 million a year...

The Reagan administration rewards its supply-side friends not just with tax breaks, but with bargain-basement prices for resources (above all land, coal, oil, and lumber); and by purchasing war commodities on a stupendous scale at extravagant prices.

Watt's legacy is enduring. He gave oil and gas companies a 5-year opportunity to lease virtually all offshore land under U.S. coastal waters — 1 billion acres, "more than ten times the amount of offshore acreage offered for oil exploration leasing in the entire history of the U.S.!" (Lou Cannon)

YOU WASCALLY WABBIT! I WON'T LEAVE A TWEE STANDING TILL I FIND YOU!

Watt also leased three times more onshore land for oil and gas exploration than Carter did. In 1982 alone, Watt sold mining companies leases to 1.7 billion tons of governmental coal. The director of the Bureau of Land Management said approvingly that Watt had converted the Bureau into a "one-stop shopping" center for the mining industry.

The tale of Watt's kindness to business is too vast and varied for detailed recounting here. But consider one typical item...

Does the term "giveaway" seem too strong? In December, 1981, Shell Oil offered $15.2 million for an offshore oil tract; Gulf Oil made a $14.29 million bid for three similar tracts. Both bids were rejected. 17 months later, after Watt had changed the bidding rules, Shell and Gulf got what they wanted — for a total of $16.92 million *less* than the rejected 1981 bids...

The social result of Watt's extremism? Violence to the environment — with potentially irreversible consequences.

"No American wants the arms race to continue, believe me."

Has the Democratic party capitalized on Watt's departure to undo his mischief? Just the contrary. In December, 1983, the Audobon Society and seven other national groups compared Tip O'Neill and other key Democrats...to James Watt. Said the director of the League of Conservation Voters: "...the average Democrat is for the pork barrel in any way, shape, or form." Pushing water for Big Business is a two-party effort...

Making the world dangerous for
democracy — and everything else — is the heart of Reagan's foreign policy. Here, too, the supply side cashes in.

Unintentionally echoing Nazi Marshal Hermann Goering, Reagan once declared: "We must have more guns and less butter." How many more guns? The defense numbers got out of control," David Stockman reports. "They got a blank check." Reagan urged the largest peacetime arms buildup ever — $1.6 *trillion* in war dollars over five years...

Military spending rose 48% from 1981 through 1983 (after inflation). The 1984 war budget ($264 billion) exceeds the 1981 war budget by $104 billion. Through 1989, Reagan projects another 73% rise in war spending. "It's just more of the same," said a senior Pentagon official. "Much more."

Typically, Reagan's kindness to the Pentagon serves Men with Gold as well as top brass. Vast war spending gives business a nearly insatiable customer for its most expensive products. The result: pumped up profits.

Profits rise even higher when the Pentagon permits superinflated arms prices, a frequent practice. Said Stockman: "...there's a kind of swamp of $10 to $20 to $30 billion worth of waste..."

The Navy, e.g., buys tape recorders at 47 times the usual price. The Air Force spends $9600 to buy a 12¢ Allen wrench, $7410 to buy a 3" wire pin worth pennies, and $1485 to buy an ordinary $5 wrench. Plastic caps for chair legs have brought in as much as $1000 each.

On average, the inflation rate for weapons systems (20% in 1981) is double that for commodities in general.

Nuclear weapons now in existence have 100,000 times the explosive power of all World War II weapons — the equivalent of three tons of dynamite for every person alive. A single Trident submarine carries enough firepower to destroy every major city in the northern hemisphere.

Worldwide, most nuclear firepower is American. Is this enough? Not for Reagan. For years Reagan has represented a faction of the business class which seeks unquestioned U.S. global supremacy. Late in 1976, irritated with Trilateralism, this faction founded the Committee on the Present Danger (CPD). Ronald Reagan is a CPD director — as are many of his top appointees, past and present:

7000% overkill (?)

Secretary of State George Shultz; CIA director William Casey; Navy chief John Lehman; Jeane Kirkpatrick, UN Ambassador; Richard Perle, Assistant Secretary of Defense; Fred Ikle, Undersecretary of Defense for Policy; top Arms Control staff Paul Nitze, Edward Rowny, and Eugene Rostow; former National Security Adviser Richard Allen; and "the whole hierarchy" (to quote Charles Tyroler, CPD chair).

Perturbed by the Indochinese defeat and determined not to repeat it, the Present Danger faction urges very hard-line steps both against Russia and against all radical movements (which it sees as expressions of Russian influence). CPD members want U.S. business to stay on top by completely unsubtle means. Reagan is perfect for the CPD — not their creation, but an ideal representative.

The ultimate CPD goal is not nuclear parity but a new springtime for U.S. strength — dominance so overwhelming that the U.S. will be able to intervene anywhere in the world without fear of Soviet retaliation. Carter/Brzezinski took steps in this direction; Reagan takes giant strides.

"Russia is still enemy number one."

"How do you compromise with men who say we have no soul...?"

"War was declared a hundred years ago by Karl Marx and...there can only be one end...victory or defeat."

FOUNTAIN OF EUTHANASIA

"The Soviet Union underlies all the unrest that is going on. If they weren't engaged in this game of dominos, there wouldn't be any hot spots in this world." So Ronald Reagan told the *Wall Street Journal* in 1980.

As a theory of world politics this has little to recommend it. Would there be no South African tumult over apartheid without Soviet meddling? No Irish resistance — after 200 years? No Central American revolutions amid great poverty and oppression? For Reagan, apparently, the answer is *yes*. Reagan subscribes to a demonology in which the Soviet Union is "the focus of evil in the modern world" (as he said in 1982). His 1980 and 1976 press secretary confirms that, "on the question of Russians and Communism, Ronald Reagan is a true believer, no doubt about it."

Present Danger ideologues want to intimidate the Soviet Union above all else. Says Richard Perle: "I've always worried less about what would happen in an actual nuclear exchange than...an American president feeling he cannot afford to take action in a crisis [for fear of] Soviet nuclear forces..."

Rostow and others agree: the "present danger" is that the U.S. will feel reluctant to crush new Vietnams. To dispel this reluctance, Reaganauts are willing to risk World War III...

"No more Vietnams, no more Taiwans." This Reagan slogan encapsulates his Third World agenda. Indochina infuriated Reagan. "The plain truth of the matter is that we were there to counter the master plan of the communists for world conquest..."

For Reagan, the Vietnam war was "a noble cause" which should not have been lost. He urged "a declaration of war on North Vietnam. We could invade the place, pave it over, and be home for lunch." A Reagan aide later said the best idea would have been to put "90% of the country under water" by bombing the North Vietnamese dikes.

Reagan also explicitly urged the use of "any and all weapons up to and including tactical nuclear bombs." For Reagan, WWIII fears are a sign of weakness. He wants "...what we fully expect will not be a warlike showdown, but a political face-off in which the Soviet Union and the other communist nations will realize that...if they push it any farther, they'll have to confront us nose to nose..." When push comes to shove, Reagn expects the Soviet Union to back down. That's the theory, anyway...

At various times Reagan has plumped for an "eyeball to eyeball" confrontation with Angola, Ecuador, North Korea, Iran, etc. In 1975, criticizing Gerald Ford over the Panama Canal issue, Reagan's rhetoric grew so sulphuric that even Barry Goldwater dissented — accusing Reagan of "a surprisingly dangerous state of mind, which is that he will not seek alternatives to a military solution when dealing with complex foreign policy issues."

Reagan's strategic objective is clear — to "roll back communism," meaning both Soviet power and popular revolutions. In May, 1982, the White House acknowledged "a campaign aimed at internal reform in the Soviet Union and shrinkage of the Soviet empire." 82-year-old Laurence Beilenson, former SAG general counsel and now Reagan's foreign policy mentor, takes a radical stance: "We ought to try to overthrow any Communist government. I go all the way. I include Yugoslavia...I'd try to overthrow the government of China, too.

Then-Secretary of State Haig termed this "the Perle-Weinberger line," which he summarized tersely: "Anything Marxist is evil and must be destroyed. The Soviet Union is ready to collapse and if we just apply a few more sanctions, it will."

Though Haig expressed unease about "brittle confrontational policies the outcome of which we might not be prepared to face," still, when the opportunity arose (in El Salvador) he pressed forward with just such policies...

The Empire Strikes Back

It seems likely that Reagan's adventurism thus far is mild compared to what he might do in a second term. It is mild, however, only by Reaganite standards. Carter's 200,000-troop Rapid

Deployment Force (RDF) has doubled in size with Reagan in office (receiving $4 billion in yearly funding and $20 billion for special enhancements). In 1982, Reagan also formed a Special Operations Command to supply U.S. allies with training in "guerrilla operations, sabotage, and terror."

Reagan's special operations test case has been Central America...

Nicaragua, El Salvador

Guatemala, and Honduras have been invaded by the U.S. many times. In 1935, conscience-stricken Marine General Smedley Butler confessed that he had been "...a high-class muscle man for big business, for Wall Street...I helped purify Nicaragua for the international banking house of Brown Brothers in 1909-12. I helped rape half a dozen Central American republics. I helped make Mexico safe for American oil interests in 1914. I helped save Haiti and Cuba for the National Bank boys..."

After stopping rebels led by Augusto Sandino, U.S. troops left Nicaragua in 1933 (following several 1920's invasions). 1933 was also crucial for neighboring El Salvador — the year of the great *Matanza,* massacre, in which General Hernandez Martinez presided over the slaughter of 30,000 insurgent workers and peasants.

Explains the unflappable Jeane Kirkpatrick: "To many Salvadorans the violence of this repression seems less important than the fact of restored order..." No doubt! Indeed, some order-loving Salvadorans now belong to "traditionalist death squads that pursue revolutionary activists and...call themselves Hernandez Martinez Brigades..."

In both Nicaragua and El Salvador intense resistance to dictatorship and exploitation percolated to the surface in the 1970's...

In Nicaragua, the regime of Anastasio Somoza was legendary for its greed and brutality. Profoundly hated, Somoza remained in power only by the grace of U.S. support.

Still, despite lavish funding, Somoza's National Guard was unable to prevent the rise of the vastly popular Sandinista Liberation Front. Towards the end, Somoza grew desperate, trying to terrorize the Nicaraguan public with indiscriminate bombing. He failed. The Sandinistas took power in 1979.

Though far from perfect, the Sandinistas are infinitely better than any previous Nicaraguan leadership. Dedicated to literacy and improved living standards, the Sandinistas are a far cry from the rapacious rulers of Guatemala, El Salvador, Chile, etc.

They are also light-years from the "communist dictatorship armed to the teeth" that Reagan raves about. Although *not* democratic enough — with a tendency to restrict popular self-rule — the Sandinistas are *not* one-party rulers. Opposition is permitted. Neither workers nor capitalists are denied all access to power. (In fact, capitalists retain far more power than many workers would like.)

This, then, is the regime against which Reagan has chosen to mount an increasingly brazen war drive. In November, 1981, Reagan authorized the CIA to undertake anti-Sandinista operations. The consequence has been the largest CIA effort since the Vietnam war. 15,000 *contras* (counterrevolutionaries) have been hired as mercenaries. Most are former National Guardsmen. Their tactic: terrorism.

In 1982-83 a total of $81 million in avowed CIA funding subsidized raids on villages, oil depots, airports, and industry; bombings and rocket attacks; the burning of sugar fields; assassination attempts; etc.

In 1984, the CIA added harbor minings to its Nicaraguan repertoire.

All this — to overthrow a popular government...

Reagan's "justification" for his war against Nicaragua is alleged Cuban/Nicaraguan support for the revolution in El Salvador — support the Salvadoran revolution completely merits, but which (apparently) has been negligible.

The Salvadoran Revolution: In April, 1983, Reagan complimented Carter: "Near the end of his presidency, Carter responded to a guerrilla offensive with a prompt supply of arms and ammunition. The guerrilla offensive failed but not America's will." In September, Carter returned the compliment: though the Salvadoran government is "one of the most bloodthirsty, perhaps in the world," Carter still "agrees with the administration that it is proper...to support the Salvadoran government" (AP summary).

Few situations are as straightforward as the Salvadoran war. "To an extent unusual even in Latin America," admits Kirkpatrick, "El Salvador has been dominated by a relatively small aristocracy..." Called the "Tom Thumb of the Americas" by Chilean poet Gabriela Mistral, tiny El Salvador is the industrial heart of Central America. When superexploited Salvadoran workers and peasants tried to organize politically in the 1970's, they were greeted by a wave of repression so rabid that the 1933 *Matanza* was soon eclipsed...

A CAST OF THOUSANDS

To date, nearly 50,000 Salvadorans have been murdered by death squads called "fascist" even by Reagan's envoy. Ultra-right leader Roberto D'Aubuisson acknowledges that the death squads come from the Salvadoran army. D'Aubuisson should know. With Nicholas Carranza, head of the Treasury Police, D'Aubuisson is widely regarded as the death squad organizer.

The U.S. has been unstinting in its support for Salvadoran terror. Despite polls showing massive opposition to U.S. involvement, Congress sent a total of $1.157 billion to Central America in 1982-83. $260.3 million went to El Salvador. In 1984, Reagan's advisory group proposed $700 million in Salvadoran military aid through 1985.

This is open public spending. Recently, a government official also confirmed that the CIA secretly pays Nicholas Carranza $90,000 a year.

The arc of U.S. involvement in El Salvador is clear. Along with firepower, the U.S. has supplied military training and, lately (to prevent imminent victory by the popular Salvadoran rebels), day-to-day leadership. Starting June 10, 1983, the Salvadoran army began taking orders from six senior U.S. strategists who met daily with the Salvadoran High Command. A Vietnam-style "pacification campaign" was initiated. Preceded by A-37 Dragonfly bombers, 6000 Salvadoran troops tried to resettle people in the central provinces into "strategic hamlets." Field teams of U.S. advisers entered combat headquarters throughout El Salvador, with Col. John Waghelstein of the U.S. "Milgroup" (Military Group) in overall command.

A total of 100+ U.S. troops are now in El Salvador. Two thousand more are stationed in Honduras, where a permanent training center, "assault airstrips," and an 11-mile tank trap have been constructed at Puerto Castillo. Aerial reconnaissance flights from the 9000-troop U.S. Southern Command in Panama supply intelligence, while big military exercises bring aircraft carriers, destroyers, and up to 33,000 U.S. troops into the region.

Three Reagan canards deserve quick refutation: that U.S. military aid is justified by "improved human rights;" that the rebel FMLN is "also responsible" for death squad murders; and that the Salvadoran government is freely elected.

Fact: The Roman Catholic Archdiocese of San Salvador confirmed an *increase* in death squad murders in the second half of 1983 — from 211 to 218 per month. *Fact:* Amnesty International and other observers agree that revolutionaries are almost entirely the victims, not the agents, of death squad terror. Winning in the field, the FMLN is famous for releasing captured troops — troops the government then considers potentially subversive and will not redeploy. *Fact:* The Salvadoran government makes failure to vote a criminal offense; votes are plainly visible on thin paper ballots in lucite ballot boxes; and candidates who whisper pro-labor or anti-military sentiments wind up dead. So much for "democracy."

Despite U.S. efforts, the Salvadoran revolution is clearly winning. The pacification campaign failed. With Salvadoran troops demoralized and ineffective, the danger of U.S. intervention grows daily. Reagan set a precedent for this in Grenada...

Grenada is a tiny Caribbean island with an English-speaking Black population of 110,000 which, in early 1979, underwent the start of a social revolution. Maurice Bishop's New Jewel Movement (NJM) ousted a corrupt regime headed by Eric Gairy and the feared Mongoose Gang. An impressive series of reforms went into effect. The New Jewel Movement won great public confidence.

Nevertheless, Bishop and the NJM failed to share top-level deliberation with the public. Thus, in October, 1983, when a violent faction fight broke out at the top of the NJM, the Grenadan public was caught off guard and Reagan saw an ideal opportunity to invade. A rival leader had arrested, then executed charismatic Maurice Bishop. Stunned, the angry Grenadian population was unwilling to protect Bishop's killer. Reagan sent in the Marines. In the months that followed, NJM gains were radically reversed.

The Grenada invasion also diverted public attention from the bombing in Lebanon — which had shaken Reagan just days earlier...

Lebanon is central to Reagan's Mideast policy: hard-line support for Israeli expanisionism and opposition to the Palestine Liberation Organization (PLO). In 1983, with U.S. backing, Israel drove the PLO out of Lebanon. But securing Lebanon proved to be another matter. After Israel withdrew to Southern Lebanon, Reagan decided to fill the vacuum in Beirut with U.S. troops. His object: to defend the governing right-wing Phalangists — originally an avowedly Fascist party — from left-leaning pro-Palestinian forces.

This plan quickly proved short-sighted, however, as Reagan swam out of his depth into the Byzantine cross-currents of Lebanese politics. Lacking a clear agenda, Reagan's "peace-keeping force" stumbled from one misstep to another. Finally, when 250+ U.S. servicemen were blown up by a Muslim anti-Phalangist, Reagan could find no alternative to withdrawal. No clear purpose had been served by U.S. intervention.

Elsewhere, too, Reagan has shown an appetite for careless military adventurism: shooting down Libyan planes; sending AWACS jets, Red-Eye rocket launchers, and $25 million to an unpopular regime in Chad; ending the embargo on arms aid to Guatemala, etc. Dangers of war do not seem to haunt Reagan...

Reagatomics: Apocalypse Now?

"I fear that what some Europeans are predicting will come to pass: that all of Europe and Western Asia will unite in a grand socialist alliance in the next 10 or 15 years..." This is a central Reagan anxiety. Like T.S. Eliot, Reagan fears that Western traditions may end "not with a bang, but with a whimper." Reagan resolves "to show Europe that we have no intention of leaving the pages of history with a whimper..'

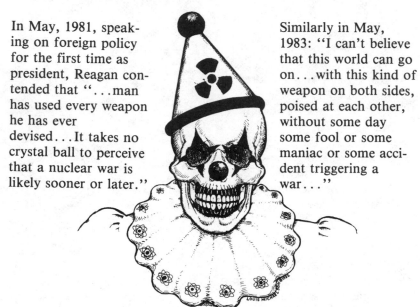

In May, 1981, speaking on foreign policy for the first time as president, Reagan contended that "...man has used every weapon he has ever devised...It takes no crystal ball to perceive that a nuclear war is likely sooner or later."

Similarly in May, 1983: "I can't believe that this world can go on...with this kind of weapon on both sides, poised at each other, without some day some fool or some maniac or some accident triggering a war..."

Reagan also seems to believe that Armageddon is near. Shortly after the Beirut bombing Reagan told a supporter:

"You know, I turn back to your ancient prophets in the Old Testament and the signs foretelling Armageddon, and I find myself wondering if — if we're the generation that is going to see that come about."

Evangelical Christians are surely entitled to views of this kind, but a U.S. president has the power to *make* Armageddon real. Is it comforting to think that Reagan might view nuclear war as a confirmation of his religious ideas?

Defense Secretary Weinberger and James Watt have expressed similar feelings. *Weinberger:* "I have read the Book of Revelation and, yes, I believe the world is going to end — by an act of God, I hope — but every day I think that time is running out..."

Watt: "I do not know how many future generations we can count on before the Lord returns."

Reagan seems to feel that the present generation may be among the last: "There have been times in the past when we thought the end of the world was coming, but never anything like this." Ominous!

Freud once wrote a book on Woodrow Wilson in which he explained his "antipathy" for Wilson by arguing that "a man who is capable of taking the illusions of religion so literally" is "unfitted" for serious decision-making.

Once, Reagan indicated that psychoanalysis holds no terrors for him: "Well, you know, a headshrinker, he's probably sitting there looking at the pupils of my eyes on television. He can see me on the couch now. Well, I want to tell you, if I get on that couch, it will be to take a nap."

Reagan shows an unseemly enthusiasm for weapons. A supporter of Truman's decision to level two Japanese cities with atomic bombs, Reagan recalls with excitement "the announcement of a fantastic bomb that had just fallen on Hiroshima." A gun collector, Reagan enthuses about the cruise missile: "You can shoot it down a pickle barrel at 2000 miles."

TYRANOSAURUS MX

About the MX Reagan quips: "Some of my best friends are MX missiles." As if to prove the point, close friend Ed Meese chimes in with a joke: Why is the MX like a Hallmark greeting card? Because if we go to war, we want to send the very best.

About the Neutron bomb Reagan talks in glowing terms:

"Very simply it is the dreamed-of death ray weapon of science fiction. It kills enemy soldiers but doesn't blow up the surrounding countryside or destroy villages, towns, and cities."

The president entrusted with jurisdiction over these weapons is a football fanatic — something very ordinary in itself, but expressed by Reagan in revealing terms: "Football is the last thing left in civilization where two men can literally fling themselves bodily at one another and not be at war. It's a kind of clean hatred..."

"I know of no other game that gave me the same feeling football did. That's why you can look at the bench when the TV camera comes over and see the fellows crying. I've sat there crying."

DON'T LOOK AT ME THAT WAY!

Reagan is far more positive about arms than about arms negotiations. Two key associates, Assistant Defense Secretary Perle and Assistant Secretary of State Burt, oppose arms treaties on principle. Jeane Kirkpatrick sneeringly dismisses "the most farfetched phenomena — unicorns, witches, universal disarmament..."

Paul Nitze, the chief arms negotiator — and co-founder of the Present Danger group with Eugene Rostow — pours cold water on the idea of negotiations: "There *could* be serious arms control negotiations, but only after we have built up our forces." When would that be? "In ten years."

181

Actually, the Neutron bomb is just a hydrogen bomb which destroys *less* property per person than the average nuclear weapon. Reagan's ignorance here is characteristic.

SPACE CADET RAYGUN REPORTING FOR DUTY, SIR. LASER WARFARE, THAT'S THE TICKET!

Eisenhower's science advisor, Kistiakowsky, and former CIA deputy director Scoville issued a statement calling Reagan "far less informed on nuclear weapons...than any president since the nuclear age began."

What one critic calls "nothing less than a conscious commitment to beat our plowshares into swords" entails many specifics, including: plans for 8458 cruise missiles; 1300 Neutron bombs; the deployment of 572 land-based missiles in Western Europe; the production of 100 MX missiles — each 71 feet long, weighing 195,000 pounds, and equipped with 10 nuclear warheads; renewed nerve gas production, after a 14 year moratorium; secret nuclear testing, renewed after a seven year hiatus;

and plans for 'Star Wars' lasers designed to attack nuclear weapons from space (a bargain at just $27 billion)...

182

In 1950, Nitze drafted a cynical paper for Truman urging the false *appearance* of a desire for arms control, where "U.S. leaders would constantly put forth reasonable-sounding disarmament proposals which the Soviets were unlikely to accept" (*Washington Post* summary).

Eugene Rostow, Reagan's first Arms Control director, believes that "...we are living in a pre-war and not a post-war world."

The 1980 Republican platform explicitly urges "overall military and technological superiority over the Soviet Union." This sounds less like a call for *closing* "the window of vulnerability" than for opening one into the Soviet Union. In a clearly inferior situation, the Soviet Union might be tempted to strike first — to pre-empt an expected U.S. first strike.

Expecting a U.S. first strike would not be unreasonable, since the MX, the Pershing 2, the Trident 2, and the D-5 (not yet deployed) all boast the capacity to penetrate hardened nuclear silos with deadly accuracy.

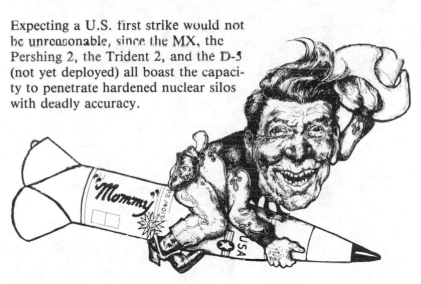

Says Kistiakowsky with irrefutable logic: "There is no point in destroying empty silos. Therefore, clearly, we are talking about a first strike, before the Soviets have launched their ICBM's." Two former CIA directors (and many others) agree.

WARNING: THIS MAN MAY BE DANGEROUS TO YOUR HEALTH

The Defense Department has long wanted what Deputy Defense Secretary Carlucci calls "nuclear war-fighting capability." A military Field Manual from the Carter era (1980) states flatly that "The U.S. Army must be prepared to fight and win when nuclear weapons are used." And Reagan in 1981 signed a secret National Security document urging a strategy for prolonged nuclear war-fighting.

Reagan is far from the first president to contemplate a nuclear first strike — Truman, Kennedy, Johnson, Nixon, and Carter entertained similar notions. Never before, however, has so much credence been given to the idea of post-war survival. The flip side of Reagan's Armageddon fatalism seems to be a fatal optimism about post-war recovery.

T.K. Jones, Deputy Under Secretary of Defense for strategic nuclear research, projects a two-to-four year recovery from full-scale nuclear war. "If there are enough shovels to go around, everybody's going to make it." "You've got to be in a hole...The dirt really is the thing that protects you...You know, dirt is just great stuff."

Amazingly, this lunacy is common among Reaganauts. William Chipman, director of Reagan's civil defense program, answered affirmatively when asked if key institutions would survive total war. "I think they would eventually, yeah. As I say, the ants eventually build another anthill." Federal Emergency Management director Giuffrida agrees: "It would be a terrible mess, but it wouldn't be unmanageable." Rostow, Bush, and others insist that nuclear war would *not* yield common ruin for the contending parties. The IRS and the Post Office both have plans for post-war operations...

FAST FORWARD

It would be enjoyable to report that Ronald Wilson Reagan is the beginning and end of all present dangers. Evidence in plenty shows just how dangerous Reagan can be. But the woes and contradictions of present society spring from far deeper roots. No single politician or business strategy bears responsibility for more than a fraction of today's ills.

The U.S. and the U.S.S.R., Democrats and Republicans, liberals and post-liberals — all alike are implicated in a system of global, life-threatening competition. The principle of this competition is the "profit motive," i.e., the drive to accumulate capital by means of employer-controlled commodity production and exchange.

It makes no fundamental difference whether the employers who control production are private individuals, monopoly corporations, or state bureaucracies. As long as profit is the name of the game, social needs are vandalized:

• In production, people are treated as if they were costly and unruly machinery, to be rigorously controlled for the greater glory of the employer.

• More generally, production seems to be inspired by a demonic dementia — with profit rather than human need the ruling passion. The consequence is the production of weapons, toxic foods, unsafe cars, etc.

THREE MILE ISLAND?
DIDN'T NOTICE ANY
NUCLEAR LEAKAGE
ON MY VISIT!

Anything that yields a profit will be produced. As it happens, many of the most profitable commodities are also deadly — war products and tainted consumer goods. The results are well known...

Firms *compete* — nations *fight*. Trade wars spark shooting wars. War products — sought by the richest buyers — attract disproportionate investment. Employers exert power not only over firms, but over markets and governments...

The central principle of the world economy is what Marx called "production anarchy." Each firm, and each nation, looks out for itself — period. If sweet harmony results, fine. Normally, though, corporations and cooperation are antithetical. Nationalism and rationality clash. The result is a chaos of firms and nations in permanent rivalry. Prices and production are profoundly unregulated.

For complex reasons, prices and unemployment rise like helium balloons, with no employer capable of restraining them. This is where politicians enter in. Though people generally assume that the *status quo* is basically unchangeable — that production will always be for profit, with competing employers in command — it is also hoped that *maybe,* just maybe, a leader will come along with enough wisdom and magic ("the right stuff") to reverse stagflation and war trends. It is hoped that what Marx called "the Fetish economy" — the uncontrolled juggernaut which results from economic anarchy — will be tamed by the charisma of a special leader.

Time after time these hopes are disappointed — but time after time they spring eternal. Very rarely does the public recognize that, short of hypnotizing Big Business and the superpowers, political officeholders can do little more than what Keynesian economists call "fine tuning" — i.e., "moving the chairs around on the deck of the Titanic" (in the words of a former official).

Changing the overall direction of society — putting the Titanic on a better course — is vastly more difficult to achieve. No charismatic leader can coax Big Business and the superpowers to give up their evil ways. For an end to social anarchy — and its consequences, stagflation and war — a public decision is required: to produce not for profit, but for public benefit; to cooperate instead of competing.

Superpower and employer rivalries must be *stopped*— before their fallout stops us all.

My alternative? World democracy without bosses or generals — socialism in Marx's sense.

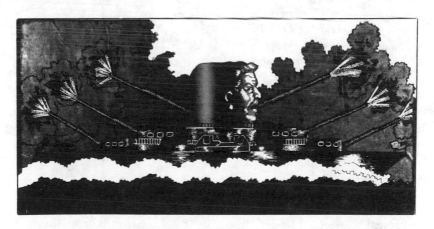

Nothing will ever be more difficult to attain — but if employers and governments are *not* stopped, they will speed us into the abyss. The choice is ours.

Only the wage-working public can take the revolutionary steps needed to move us beyond our present impasse. The vast effort this requires, however, makes the prospect seem remote. Working people feel weak and isolated. Big Business and the world economy seem irresistible. Meanwhile, Russian arms seem to justify U.S. arms (to the U.S. public) while U.S. arms legitimate Russian arms (to the Russian public). Nobody stands to win in the end — but there seems to be no way out.

With basic change seemingly ruled out, people settle for modest hopes: a job, restrained inflation, fewer wars. Enter the Demopublicans. Differing just enough to give the public a slight degree of choice, each party claims charisma for its candidates and traditions. The Demopublican promise is that, *this* time, the cycle of inflation, recession, and war danger can be reversed (at least partly). "Just vote Demopublican!"

STAND ON MY RECORD? WHAT FOR?

Typically, after a surge of hope, the public either accepts the deflation of this promise or searches for a new 'charismagician.' So far, the Demopublicans have not failed either completely or obviously enough to prompt a public rethinking of the political equation. Reagan is doing his best; but still...

It may also be the case that the public is too pessimistic or authoritarian to reject even suicidal misleadership. If apathy prevails, the public may wind up following the Demopublicans into war and economic crisis.

The same result is likely if people prove to be excessively wedded to authoritarianism. Most people identify with *something* greater than themselves. Sometimes, to compensate for feelings of personal weakness, people identify with leaders valued for their presumed "strength" rather than for their moral qualities. Reagan's support derives partly from power-worship of this type. A remarkable 1984 poll showed, for example, that well over 50% of the public "approved" Reagan's presidency — while less than 1% defined Reagan as a "compassionate" leader and just one quarter of the respondents felt that Reagan "cares about people like me."

HOW TO STAY FIT
By Ronald Reagan

Evidently, many people who are not entirely fooled by Reagan support him anyway. This support is alarming to the extent that it reveals voluntary submissivenes — at a time when resistance is vitally needed.

Death Valley Days?

Anyone who finds this analysis convincing will probably have mixed feelings. Either you'll want to (a) stop reading and never think about politics again, (b) move to the Australian bush country, (c) fight back...or all three.

Fighting back may seem like a forlorn venture with little chance of success, but (late-breaking news flash) that's life. With war and disaster on the horizon, is there an alternative? Is there a better response to tyranny than resistance?

No one can guarantee that the profound and bitter struggles of the likely mid-term future will avert crisis and holocaust. But without the widest possible effort, it is a virtual certainty that disaster will befall us. The scales *can* be tipped; every contribution helps.

Don't be too discouraged. Far more is possible — and likely — than most people imagine. Twentieth-century history shows that crisis often prompts response — and that even revolutionary change is possible. Few eras in history have witnessed comparable upheaval.

Several promising current trends deserve mention.

The giant European anti-war movement — involving tens of millions of people — is very encouraging. Few struggles have ever been so genuinely and completely international. Western *and* Eastern Europeans have taken pathbreaking steps, signaling the possibility (as well as the need) for joint East-West resistance. It seems likely that this movement will survive for some time...

In the U.S., stirrings in the Black and minority communities, among women, and in the ranks of Big Labor suggest the possibility of greater militancy and unity ("a rainbow coalition") in the not-too-distant future.

At the national level, Reagan has inspired demonstrations of unprecedented size: the "Solidarity Day" labor demonstrations and the 1983 March on Washington (commemorating the 20th anniversary of the great 1963 civil rights march). At the community level, restlessness and disaffection are clear.

The question, now, is whether disaffection will translate into sustained resistance; and whether resistance will take effectively organized forms.

It seems likely that women will play an ever more central role in future resistance. Polls recently have shown that significantly more women than men oppose militarism and inequality. If this trend continues, men will have a lot of catching up to do...

Finally, the Salvadoran and Polish examples also bear mention. The Salvadoran people have shown unmatched heroism and unity in resisting an insensate reign of terror. If the U.S. *stays out,* the Salvadoran people will almost certainly win.

In Poland, similarly, a mass movement of unprecedented breadth and depth brought workers from virtually every factory, office, and mine into one giant union, *Solidarnosc.* Defeat at the hands of the combined Soviet/Polish bureaucracy does not alter the fact that a new type of movement has been born...

As the great Polish revolutionary Rosa Luxemburg once wrote, we must be prepared to lose every battle — except the last one.

References

Thanks to the following for pictures:
Adam Cornford, Elliott Smith

Lack of space makes it impossible to document the many quotes and facts cited in this book, but readers who wish to trace a specific point can write to the author (in care of the publisher) for a reference. With the exception of a small number of punchlines in balloons, all citations in this book are genuine. For reasons of space, some citations are slightly condensed.

From the following selected bibliography, books which deserve especially wide attention include those by Frank Ackerman, Ronnie Dugger, William Greider, Robert Lekachman, Frances Fox Piven and Richard Cloward, Robert Scheer, and Laurence Shoup. Thanks to one and all for trailblazing work.

For readers who might like to become politically active, the excellent human rights directory by Christiano and Young (below) furnishes a clear and extensive list of human rights groups — and many others. *Good luck.*

Frank Ackerman. **Reaganomics: Rhetoric vs. Reality.** Boston: South End Press, 1982; Bill Boyarsky. **Ronald Reagan, His Life and Rise to the Presidency.** New York: Random House, 1981; Edmund G. (Pat) Brown and Bill Brown. **Reagan, The Political Chameleon.** New York: Praeger Publishers, 1976; Lou Cannon. **Reagan.** New York: G.P. Putnam's Sons, 1982; David Christiano and Lisa Young. **Human Rights Organizations and Periodicals Directory.** Berkeley, CA: Meiklejohn Civil Liberties Institute, P.O. Box 673, Berkeley, CA 94701, (415) 848-0599, 1983; Kathy Randall Davis. **But What's He Really Like?** U.S. Pacific Coast Publishers, 1970. Royce D. Delmatier, Clarence F. McIntosh, and Earl G. Waters, eds. **The Rumble of California Politics, 1848-1970.** New York: John Wiley and Sons Inc., 1970. Ronnie Dugger. **On Reagan: The Man and His Presidency.** New York: McGraw-Hill Book Company, 1983; James Fallows. **"Reagan: The Fruits of Success".** New York Review of Books, 10-27-83; Barry M. Goldwater. **Why Not Victory? A Fresh Look At American Foreign Policy.** New York: MacFadden, 1963; Mark Green and Gail MacColl, eds. **There He Goes Again: Ronald Reagan's Reign of Error.** New York: Pantheon, 1983; William Greider. **The Education of David Stockman and Other Americans.** New York: Dutton, 1982; Gary Hart. **A New Democracy.** New York: William Morrow and Company Inc., 1983; Charles D. Hobbs. **Ronald Reagan's Call To Action.** New York: Thomas Nelson Inc., 1976; Richard Kazis and Richard L. Grossman. **Fear at Work: Job Blackmail, Labor, and the Environment.** New York: The Pilgrim Press, 1982; Jonathan King and Steve Rees. **Poor Ronald's Almanac. A Mother Jones Magazine Sourcebook,** 1983; Jeane J. Kirkpatrick. **Dictatorship and Double Standards: Rationalism and Reason in Politics.** New York: Simon and Schuster, 1982; Frank Keifer, ed. **I Goofed: The Wise and Curious Sayings of Ronald Reagan, 33rd Governor of California.** Diablo Press, Box 7084, Berkeley, CA 94717, 1968; Michael Klare *et al.* **Myths and Realities of the 'Soviet Threat': Proceedings of an IPS Conference on U.S.-Soviet Relations.** Washington: Institute for Policy Studies, 1901 Que Street, N.W., Washington, DC. 20009 (202) 234-9382, n.d.; Robert Lekachman. **Greed Is Not Enough: Reaganomics.** New York: Pantheon Books, 1982; Joseph Lewis. **What Makes Reagan Run? A Political Profile.** New York: McGraw-Hill Book Company, 1968; Samuel Lubell. **The Future of American Politics.** New York: Harper and Row, 1965; Doug McClelland. **Hollywood on Ronald Reagan.** Winchester, Massachusetts: Faber and Faber, 1983; Frances Fox Piven and Richard A. Cloward. **The New Class War: Reagan's Attack on the Welfare State and Its Consequences.** New York: Pantheon Books, 1982; Nancy Reagan. **Nancy.** New York: William Morrow and Company Inc., 1980; Ronald Reagan. **Where's the Rest of Me?.** New York: Duell, Sloan and Pearce, 1965; Robert Scheer. **With Enough Shovels: Reagan, Bush and Nuclear War.** New York: Random House, 1983; Laurence H. Shoup. **The Carter Presidency and Beyond: Power and Politics in the 1980's.** Palo Alto, CA: Ramparts Press, 1980; Hedrick Smith, *et al.* **Reagan the Man, the President.** New York: MacMillan Publishing Co., 1980; George H. Smith. **Who is Ronald Reagan?** New York: Pyramid Books, 1968. Tony Thomas; **The Films of Ronald Reagan.** Secaucus, NJ: Citadel Press, 1980; Jude Wanniski. **The Way the World Works: How Economies Fail. . .and Succeed.** New York: Basic Books Inc., 1978; Jules Witcover. **Marathon: The Pursuit of the Presidency, 1972-1976.** New York: The Viking Press, 1977.

Typesetting lovingly done by the Krieshok sisters without ever any complaining, and in plenty of time.